RATIONAL CONSENSUS IN SCIENCE AND SOCIETY

PHILOSOPHICAL STUDIES SERIES
IN PHILOSOPHY

VOLUME 24

RATIONAL CONSENSUS
IN
SCIENCE AND SOCIETY

A Philosophical and Mathematical Study

by

KEITH LEHRER

Dept. of Philosophy, The University of Arizona, Tucson

and

CARL WAGNER

Mathematics Dept., The University of Tennessee, Knoxville

D. REIDEL PUBLISHING COMPANY

DORDRECHT : HOLLAND / BOSTON : U.S.A.

LONDON : ENGLAND

Library of Congress Cataloging in Publication Data

Lehrer, Keith.
    Rational consensus in science and society.

    (Philosophical studies series in philosophy ; v. 24)
    Bibliography: p.
    Includes index.
        1.   Science–Philosophy–Mathematical models.
    2.   Science–Social aspects–Mathematical models.   3.   Consensus
    (Social sciences)–Mathematical models.   I.   Wagner, Carl, 1943–
    II.   Title.   III.   Series.
    Q175.L4335   121   81–13764
    ISBN 90-277-1306-5   AACR2
    ISBN 90-277-1307-3 pbk. (Pallas edition)

Published by D. Reidel Publishing Company,
P.O. Box 17, 3300 AA Dordrecht, Holland.

Sold and distributed in the U.S.A. and Canada
by Kluwer Boston Inc.,
190 Old Derby Street, Hingham, MA 02043, U.S.A.

In all other countries, sold and distributed
by Kluwer Academic Publishers Group,
P.O. Box 322, 3300 AH Dordrecht, Holland.

D. Reidel Publishing Company is a member of the Kluwer Group.

Printed in the Netherlands

Dedicated with appreciation and respect
to our teachers Wilfrid Sellars and Leonard Carlitz

TABLE OF CONTENTS

PREFACE

This book is the joint project of a philosopher, Lehrer, and a mathematician, Wagner. The book is, therefore, divided into a first part written by Lehrer, which is primarily philosophical, and a second part written by Wagner that is primarily formal. The authors were, however, influenced by each other throughout. Our book articulates a theory of rational consensus in science and society. The theory is applied to politics, ethics, science, and language. We begin our exposition with an elementary mathematical model of consensus developed by Lehrer in a series of articles [1976a, 1976b, 1977, 1978]. Chapter 3 contains material from [1978]. Lehrer formulated the elementary model when he was a Fellow of the Center for Advanced Study in the Behavioral Sciences, Stanford, in 1973 with the invaluable mathematical assistance of Kit Fine, Gerald Kramer and Lionel McKenzie. In the summer of 1977, Lehrer and Wagner met at the Center in a Summer Seminar on Freedom and Causality supported by the Andrew W. Mellon Foundation. Wagner read the manuscript of Lehrer [1978] and subsequently solved some mathematical problems of the elementary model. After discussions of philosophical problems associated with that model, Wagner developed the foundations for the extended model. These results were reported in Wagner [1978, 1981a]. Wagner then pursued the project as Fellow of the Center in 1978–79. Lehrer's research at the Center was supported by the American Council of Learned Societies, the University of Rochester, and the University of Arizona. His subsequent research was supported by the National Endowment for the Humanities. Wagner's research at the Center was supported by the Andrew W. Mellon Foundation, the National Science Foundation, and the University of Tennessee.

This project was the creation of the Center for Advanced Study in the Behavioral Sciences. It was conceived, sustained, and developed at the Center. It is our pleasure to express our gratitude to that extraordinary institution.

K. L.
C. W.

PART ONE

A PHILOSOPHICAL THEORY OF RATIONAL CONSENSUS

CHAPTER ONE

CONSENSUS AND PHILOSOPHICAL ISSUES

Various atomistic and individualistic theories of knowledge, language, ethics and politics have dominated philosophical thought from time to time. Such theories have not, however, proven to be adequate. One discovers and re-discovers that some social factor, some factor of agreement or consensus, whether explicitly contractual or implicitly presupposed, is necessary for an explication or explanation of some central or fundamental conception. Our intention is to offer a formal model of social consensus. We believe that our formal articulation of a conception of consensus is an advance over earlier efforts. It enables us to give a precise theory of rational consensus and an exact specificaiton of logical consequences. The formal model will be presented in two parts. First, we shall present a mechanical method or procedure, mathematically speaking, an algorithm, for finding a rational consensus from an initial starting point or input. We shall explore the application of this method to find consensual probabilities, utilities and weights. Our method will then be applied to some traditional philosophical problems concerning democracy, justice, science and language. Following this presentation, we will represent our methodology from an axiomatic point of view. In this second part, we shall formulate axioms as conditions of rational consensus and explain how our method satisfies those conditions. It will be useful, at the outset, to illustrate in some detail the fundamental role of the concept of consensus in a variety of philosophical problems. We shall begin with the most obvious applications, in politics and ethics, and then turn to less obvious applications, in science and language.

1. POLITICS

In politics, there is a tradition that attempts to justify government in terms of consensus. This tradition takes a variety of forms and has been employed to justify both dictatorial and democratic forms of government. These theories are primarily identified with Hobbes [1651], Rousseau [1762], Locke [1690b] and Spinoza [1677]. The tradition rests on the assumption that there is some principle of reason that commits men to agree to accept some form of government. The principle of reason may be one according to which all men must accept a dictator to keep the peace among them or one according to which men delegate their authority to a sovereign. What is central is the appeal to both reason and consensus. It is often quite unclear, according to these theories, how one is to ascertain a rational consensus, or, on the contrary, it is sometimes all too clear that the author projects his own individual preference and conviction as the rational consensus all men must accept in the light of reason. What is traditionally missing is a convincing account of how reason can yield consensus. When people disagree, how are we to decide what consensus is rational?

The traditional method for answering this question is to postulate some principle of reason, which, as a matter of fact, is not generally accepted, and then claim that all are committed to a consensus because they are committed to the principle. For example, one might claim, as Locke [1690] did, that everyone has a natural right to life, liberty and property. It is clear that this principle is controversial, for example, communists deny that everyone has a natural right to property. Similarly, those who cherish conflict, and there are many such, are by no means inclined to accept as a principle of reason that everyone should desire peace and security. A philosopher who enjoys the pleasures of cogitation and speculation, who is content grinding lenses the rest of the time, might well lay it down as a fundamental principle of reason that everyone should desire peace and security. Another sort of person, an adventurer who relishes danger and risk, who prefers military arts to domestic crafts, may well demure. Such principles of rationality, no matter how well favored by philosophers, cannot be rationally imposed. Instead, if these principles are to provide a rational basis for accepting government and the products thereof, they must themselves be rationally consensual.

2. SOCIAL CHOICE

It is clear that two very important recent books, one by Arrow [1951] and the other by Rawls [1971], have had such a great impact on contemporary thought that it is appropriate to mention them at the outset if only to indicate in a preliminary way the relation of our work to theirs. We shall discuss Arrow in more detail subsequently. Our axiomatic approach to social choice follows the tradition initiated by Arrow. Both Rawls and Arrow restrict the information that may be applied to reach a consensus more sharply than we do, that is, our methodology permits the aggregation of greater information.

Arrow articulated, in an especially lucid manner, the problem of amalgamating individual preferences in society in order to arrive at a social choice of policy for the group. His early work [1951] contained an impossibility theorem showing that a very plausible set of conditions for making such choices could not possibly be satisfied. Subsequent work has been devoted to considering how these conditions might be weakened so that some satisfiable rule for amalgamating individual preferences for social choice could be articulated. The work of Sen [1977] surveys these attempts. Arrow's conditions in his early work imply that *only* individual preferences among pairs of alternatives may be considered. These conditions thus restrict the *information* that may be amalgamated to reach a social choice.

An individual may have other information that he considers to be relevant. For example, if he regards a large percentage of the group to be incompetent or prejudiced and, moreover, has supporting evidence, then he might well be disinclined to commit himself to a social choice that amalgamates the preferences of such individuals. In short, preferences can be unreasonable, they can also be known to be so, and one who has such knowledge cannot be expected to be committed to a choice arrived at by ignoring such knowledge.

We do not intend these remarks as a general criticism of Arrow's early work, as our own approach is indebted to his axiomatic approach to social choice. Moreover, Arrow's recent writing [1977] appears less restrictive with respect to the informational base amalgamated in social choice. Our approach to social choice is to be viewed as an extension of Arrow's methods so that information about the reliability and expertise of others may be amalgamated with information about preference to obtain social choice.

3. JUSTICE

The theory advanced by Rawls differs more greatly from our own. According to Rawls [1971], it is not sufficient to simply amalgamate individual preferences if a social policy is to be just. Instead, the individual preferences must be arrived at in a special way, behind a veil of ignorance, that disallows an individual to base his preferences on knowledge of his special situation. Rawls then argues that such preferences should be based on a maximin policy and, therefore, that one is committed to a social policy that provides a reasonable security level for those in the society who possess the least. This representation is, of course, a simplification of a complex argument, but the details of the presentation are not relevant to our critical purposes. Our objection is easy enough to anticipate. It is unclear why an individual who is not committed to a maximin policy, perhaps because he is a devil may care type of individual who prefers a daring life to a secure one, should be committed to a social policy based on a maximin principle. Moreover, even if he is committed to a maximin policy, it is not clear why he should be committed to a policy based on a pretended ignorance of facts that are known to him and which are, in his opinion, relevant to his personal preferences. Perhaps Rawls believes that all reasonable men who read his work will accept his basic principles, and, in that case, of course, they would be committed to the policy he enunciates. However, the really voluminous criticism of Rawls attests to the fact that it is not obvious that a reasonable person is committed to those principles. People are only rationally committed to the theory of justice Rawls defends *if* they are similarly committed to the application of the veil of ignorance and maximin strategies. What is needed, and what we seek to supply, is a theory of *rational* consensus and commitment when, in fact, there is dissensus.

It is important here to clarify our position. Notice that we, in our criticism of Rawls, do not claim that the social policy derived from his principles would be unreasonable. Strasnick [1976] defends such principles by modifying Arrow. What we claim is that Rawls fails to *show* that the individuals in a society are consensually committed to the principles in question. There may, of course, be a consensus to the principles and, in that case, the individuals are rationally committed to the policy as a consequence of consensus. What is required, however, is a theory of when and how individuals are rationally committed to such a consensus.

Thus, Rawls represents an ancient tradition in ethics and political theory of implicitly laying down some principle as a principle of rationality and then claiming that we are all committed to that principle. His theory, like those proposed by his reknowned predecessors, contains substantitive presuppositions, assumptions that are only rationally binding if, in some sense, all men are consensually committed to those assumptions. We must, however, be able to decide when people *are* rationally committed to principles as a matter of social consensus. It is notable that these authors appeal to the intuitions of their readers, which is, perhaps, an implicit appeal to common sense, or common sense under the scrutiny of reflective cogitation. We believe that this is an implicit appeal to consensus, an implicit assumption that the readers will agree to what the authors aver. Our concern is to make explicit the methodology that lies behind these appeals and assumptions.

The appeal to some sort of consensus, whether actual or implicit, is familiar in ethics and political philosophy even if an explicit methodology for finding such a consensus has not been provided. In philosophy of science and epistemology, on the contrary, it has often been assumed that social factors, such as consensus, are quite irrelvant. There is, of course, some appeal to social acceptance, but it is often assumed that this is a mere symptom rather than a source of rationality. There is in both ethics and epistemology a strong *individualistic* tradition, and it is not at all surprising that such a tradition invades both fields together. The fundamental questions of both fields are verbally similar. In ethics, one asks what it is reasonable to do, what actions are justified for a person, and in epistemology one asks what it is reasonable to believe, what propositions are justified for a person. When it is held in epistemology that what it is reasonable for a person to believe does not depend on social consensus but is an entirely individual matter, it is natural enough to conclude that the same thing is true in ethics. Our claim, however, is that such individualistic accounts are incorrect in both domains. Rationality in both science and ethics rests upon rational consensus.

4. EPISTEMOLOGY

Let us consider epistemology. Suppose a philosopher articulates some epistemic principle, some rule of evidence or method of rational acceptance. To the one who advocates such a principle, rule or method, it's rationality may seem quite independent of the opinion of others, and their agreement or disagreement may appear a matter of indifference. The rationality of the principle, rule or method may seem pure and unsullied by the exigencies of interpersonal relations. We contend, however, that the principle, rule or method appears so to the person in question because of *his* commitment to it. Given his commitment to such a precept, the consequences are endowed with the rationality of consistency. Given commitment to a precept, what follows is embued with the demand of an imperative. If, however, others find his precept uncompelling, he will be chagrined to discover that they look upon him as a chauvinist and a dogmatist, one who espouses controversial opinions as though they were endowed with *a priori* necessity. Of course, he may be correct, the others may be in error, but it by no means follows they are in any way irrational. What is perfectly correct can *appear* to be erroneous, and it can be entirely reasonable to believe that it is erroneous. Consequently, it would be in no way irrational to demure. Thus, if another is to be rationally committed to a precept, in ethics or in science, he must, in some way, be consensually committed to the precept and to the results derived therefrom. The correctness of a precept or proposition may not depend on consensus, but the *rationality* of accepting that precept or proposition does. If people are committed to a consensus, then they are thereby committed to results that flow from it. If they are not so committed, it may be in no way irrational for them to dissent.

The failure to recognize this point is a frequent cause of misunderstanding. When one person advances some position, whether in ethics, science, politics or more mundane matters of everyday life, and feels fully committed to what he avers, those who demure may appear unreasonable, unfair, unappreciative and so forth. But the problem is often not what it appears to be. The position advanced, and the arguments given, may from a certain point of view, that is, given certain presuppositions, appear perfectly evident. However, when one does not share the point of view, when one is not committed to the presuppositions in question, then neither will one be committed to the results. If a consensus is to be reached, if both parties to a dispute are to be rationally committed to an outcome, they must start with some rational consensus that serves as the basis for the further argumentation.

5. SCIENCE

Science is, perhaps, the most interesting test case for our claim because in science consensus is often thought to be merely a byproduct of a rational methodology. For example, one may hold that a certain form of experimental method is the rational basis for evaluating theories and hypotheses. Agreement over hypotheses and theories, one may then aver, results from the fact that the same experimental results are obtained by different experimenters. It is clear, we suggest, that this claim is an oversimplification of actual science. Scientists, in fact, disagree about experimental outcomes, obtain different results, and, moreover, disagree over which methods are appropriate. All this might be explained in terms of the usual human failings, and it might, therefore, be contended that the methods, if properly understood and applied, would, indeed, yield the same results. We think that work in the history of science casts considerable doubt upon this sanguine empiricist account of science, but that is not the primary ground of our disagreement.

Our contention is a very simple one, to wit, that the scientists must also be consensually committed to a method. If they are not so committed, then, no matter what the intrinsic merits of the method, agreement is not to be expected. Again, if one is not rationally committed to a method, then one is not committed to the results obtained, no matter how constant and consistent those results might be. History bears this out. When others looked through Galileo's telescope, they did not by any means agree that the moons of Jupiter were there to be seen. They saw them not. It is, we suggest, moot to dispute whether they really saw the moons but denied this, or whether they did not interpret what they saw as moons. They were not committed to Galileo's methods, and, therefore, they were not committed to his claim. When we claim that the results of science are rational, when we prefer those results to prejudice and superstition, the rationality of our claim rests ultimately upon our agreement, our consensus, that those methods lead us to truth or at least expose error in a reliable way. The application of method may itself produce agreement, but such agreement presupposes a prior consensual commitment to the methodology itself.

6. INTUITION AND COMMON SENSE

It is especially interesting in this context to consider the tradition of appealing to intuition in philosophical argument, whether in ethics or epistemology. For, the appeal to intuition is, rather clearly, an appeal to consensus. When some philosopher claims that something is intuitive, or, on the contrary, when he claims that something is counter-intuitive, these claims rest on implicit reference to the consensual opinion of some group. When something is presented as a counter-example to a claim in ethics or epistemology, this amounts to the claim that the example is unacceptable, that is, that it would be contrary to a rational consensus.

The most explicit appeal to consensus, perhaps, comes from the philosophy of common sense. This tradition stems most notably from Locke [1690a] and Reid [1764]. The latter argued repeatedly that some opinion of the philosophers must be rejected because it was contrary to common sense, that is, to the untutored opinion of mankind. Often Reid notes that some philosophical theory conflicts with such opinion and remarks that he sides with the vulgar. Moore [1922], who adapted the philosophy of Reid to the twentieth century, defended many general as well as specific claims about the world by appeal to common sense. These are explicit appeals to consensus. When Reid or Moore attack some philosophical position on grounds of conflict with common sense, it is clear that the position attacked is contrary to received opinion. In order, therefore, for such criticism to escape the charge of begging the question, it must be implied that the author criticized is committed to the consensus, that is, that, rationally, he should be a party to the agreement. To advocate common sense is to claim that those who explicitly demure are, under the constraints of reason, committed to consensual opinion. Or perhaps the matter might be formulated in another way. If one criticizes a view on the grounds that it is contrary to common sense, or contrary to intuition, then one is appealing to some consensual opinion on the subject. If such criticism is cogent, then the consensual opinion must be reasonable. Such a claim naturally raises the question of why consensual opinion is reasonable, or of what makes it reasonable. And we shall shortly supply an answer.

Another sort of appeal to common sense occurs in the writings of epistemologists of such divergent views as Chisholm [1977] and Goodman [1955]. Chisholm constructs an epistemology which is in accord with common sense in that it is intended to yield the result that we know most of the things that we think we know. To that end, Chisholm has articulated a system of principles intended to yield the desired result. His defense of these principles is that they yield conclusions about what is evident, certain and known that are in accord with received opinion about what is evident, certain and known. In a similar way, Goodman conceives of the task of inductive logic as that of constructing a system yielding results in accord with intuition, which amounts, it seems to us, to reflective common sense. Now, it must be immediately noted that Goodman also remarks that a system need only coincide *for the most part* with intuition, and it is clear that he allows for the possibility that a philosophical theory might lead to some results that seem initially peculiar. When it is understood how well the system deals with *most* cases, that is, how well it accords with common sense, we should revise our opinion in those few cases. However, this is not a defense of dissensus, it is, instead, a less static view of consensual opinion than is employed by others, Reid, for example. That is to say, consensual opinion that exists at one time, before philosophical theory is considered, may differ in some instances with the consensual opinion that arises subsequent to the consideration of the theory. It remains true, nevertheless, that there is appeal to consensual opinion. It is consensus that validates the theory. It is assumed that such consensual opinion is a reasonable basis for evaluating theories. Once again, of course, it is necessary to ask what sort of consensus is being appealed to, and what makes it reasonable.

The whole movement of contemporary analytic philosophy appears to rest on the appeal to consensus. A philosophical theory grossly in conflict with common sense must be rejected. It is a hallmark of analytic philosophy that principles can be refuted with counterexamples, and, as we have noted, the assumption that something is a counterexample, for example, a counterexample to a theory of induction or knowledge, rests upon consensual opinion. A counterexample to a theory of induction might be an inductive inference that is permitted by the rule but which *we* could not accept. The editorial *we* represents a consensus. Similarly, when Gettier [1963] presents an example of a justified true belief that *we* would not accept as a case of knowledge, thereby claiming to refute the contention that knowledge is justified true belief, he implicitly appeals to consensus. *We* agree the example is not an instance of knowledge.

It is interesting to notice that current work in ethics contains such an appeal as well. It is probably most often noted in ethics that there is a danger in the appeal to intuition because it is implicitly an appeal to commonly received ethical assumptions. Nevertheless, when a philosopher notes that it is a consequense of an ethical theory that some act which seems to us flagrantly wrong would be right according to the theory, he expects that to be regarded as a serious objection. What seems to us to be unjust is, therefore, critical, and it is, of course, an appeal, however implicit and indirect, to consensual opinion. In ethics, one appreciates the fact that one must be careful not to demand of an ethical theory that it accord in every respect with commonly received ethics, but consensus remains, nevertheless, a basis for criticism. This sort of methodology requires, therefore, a theory of the rationality of consensual opinion as a foundation.

It is useful to notice also that not all parties to consensus receive equal credence. There is an appeal to consensus, but it is a consensus in which the opinions or evaluations of some are given greater weight. In short, the consensual opinion is a weighted opinion influenced by expertise. An adequate theory of consensus must explain how people can be committed to a consensus in which authorities with special expertise may dominate. This consideration is also relevant to the forementioned observation that such philosophers as Goodman and Rawls propose that our initial intuitions may be overridden in some cases by theoretical or systematic reflection. Those who are a party to theoretical understanding or the articulation of a system, those who really understand the theory or system, may, of course, alter their views in the light of such understanding. When they are also expert, and become more so through additional theoretical and systematic reflection, then their opinions should receive more weight in the amalgamation of opinion to find a rational consensus. A rational consensus should summarize what is known, and those who know more should, accordingly, influence the consensus more strongly than those who are less knowledgeable.

7. LANGUAGE

Similar considerations apply in the areas of social science and philosophy associated with the study of language. It is clear that the meaning, grammar and reference of language is, in some sense, determined by implicit consensus. It is sometimes said that such matters are governed by convention, though no explicit convention or rule has been explicitly agreed upon in any manner. To illustrate the point, let us consider briefly the matters of meaning and reference. In the case of a great many words, our use of those words involves, as Putnam [1973] has insisted, an implicit reference to the authority of some group of experts whose opinion will decide whether a word applies to some object or group of objects. For example, a technical word like 'molecule' is used by many people, but the question of whether certain objects are or are not molecules is decided by appeal to physical scientists. Perhaps this is also true of other words like 'water.' These cases are interesting because here the consensus over usage presupposes a consensus about who is authoritative, who is expert, in the use and application of the words in question. The fundamental appeal to consensus in the philosophy of language arises, however, from the attempt to explicate the relation between idiolects, the speech of an individual, and a communal language which transcends individual idiolects. There is, no doubt, substantial disagreement about how words are applied and about the semantic relations between words. The assumption of a common language rests, however, on an assumed commitment to a consensus. In a way, we may say that individuals delegate their individual prerogatives in the use of language to a communal consensus. They thereby agree that certain features of their idiolects are incorrect when they conflict with that consensus. What is needed is an account of this delegation. It is clear that the general form of the delegation involves one individual giving some weight to the usage of others, and, we suggest, it is the amalgamation of the weight or authority that one person assigns or proxies to another that generates the consensus and bridges the gap between diverse individual idiolects to yield the communal language. This process of delegation is complicated by the fact that extended *chains* of respect may be generated when one person respects a second, the second respects a third, and so forth. Thus, in the case of technical words, like 'molecule' for example, the person in the street may not know exactly who the relevant experts are but may give considerable weight to someone who, if not expert in science, may give considerable weight to some scientist unknown to the first person. Thus, in this way, the weight that the first person gives to another person may be indirectly conveyed to the expert. The model we shall articulate below explains how the amalgamation of such assignments of weight generates a consensual system.

8. AMALGAMATION OF INFORMATION

Our fundamental claim is that the information individuals posses, whether about language, ethics or science may rationally commit them to consensus. The form of consensus we shall defend is a rational amalgamation of the information individuals possess. We shall articulate a normative theory of consensual rationality in science and society. It is predicated on the assumption that human wisdom is worth amalgamation or aggregating to solve theoretical and practical problems. There is no assumption that such aggregation is an infallible guide to what is true or best. There is no such guide. The vicissitudes of practical action, no matter how well intentioned and informed, are blatant. In theoretical matters and empirical science, it is sometimes maintained that methodology can insulate us from error, but this position has been discredited, especially by recent historiographers of science. In questions of science as well as social policy, there are better and worse ways of proceeding, and to follow the better is the rational course. Our contention is that the course that amalgamates available information is more reasonable than one that neglects it. To say that it is more reasonable is not, however, to claim that one will inevitably obtain a satisfactory result. The commitment to using more comprehensive information in scientific and social practise is here taken as basic.

Assume that we wish to use the total information available to us. How should we proceed? At any given point in time, each of us is a repository of information. The information we possess may be more or less well regimented, or may require some special form or organization for specific purposes. When information is used to answer a question or solve a problem, disagreement or dissensus between individuals will often occur. We then confront the problem of how to aggregate the individual repositories of information in order to use the total information available in the group. In some circumstances, the most practical method might be to wait for further information to reduce or eliminate the disagreement. We cannot, however, answer the question of what the most reasonable answer is at a specific point in time by advising everyone to wait and see what happens. What happens only resolves disagreement at that later time. The question of what is rational at a specific time is not answered by subsequent developments. For those developments add new information not available originally. What answer or solution is rational at a specific time depends solely on the information available at that time. The problem is to ascertain what is rational on the basis of a determinate base of information. We shall offer a theory of rational consensus that solves this problem.

Our theory of consensual rationality is directly applicable to problems of allocating some sum among alternatives. The assignment of probabilities is one such problem. When we assign probabilities to a set of pairwise exclusive and mutually exhaustive alternatives, then we distribute values, none of which are negative, to the alternative hypotheses so that they sum to unity. Another such problem is the allocation of money to a set of alternative projects. We may assign either nothing or some positive sum of money to each alternative in such a way as to expend some initial sum. To solve such problems, where some fixed sum is to be distributed among alternatives each of which receives either some positive allocation or nothing, we propose that individual allocations to the alternatives be aggregated to obtain a consensual assignment.

The aggregation procedure we advocate for finding a consensual assignment is a weighted average of the individual assignments. The idea of using weighted arithmetic means to solve such problems is not unique. It is defended capably by Harsanyi [1976], [1977], for example. Our contribution is twofold. firstly, in the next chapter we propose an algorithm for finding the appropriate weights. In effect, our method is one that enables us to find consensual weights, derived from the information members of the group have about each other, in order to find a consensual arithmetic average of the individual assignments. Secondly, we provide, in Chapter 6, an axiomatic justification for our methodology. There we formulate four axioms, Irrelevance of Alternatives, Zero Unanimity, Label Neutrality, and Strong Label Neutrality, as conditions of adequacy of an allocation method and demonstrate that a method satisfying these conditions must be a weighted arithmetic average.

We also deal with a second sort of problem, one more closely associated with the Arrow tradition, of finding a consensual ranking of alternatives rather than a quantitative assignment for those alternatives. We start with some individual scoring of alternatives, but here the aggregation method is only intended to yield a ranking of the alternatives. Confronted with the diverse scoring of individuals, we again propose use of a weighted average of scores assigned to alternatives to obtain the social or consensual ranking. In Chapter 3, we explore methods for obtaining consensual rankings from consensual weights, and in Chapter 6 we formulate three axioms, Strong Pareto Condition, Independence of Irrelevant Alternatives, and Translation Invariance from which it follows, as shown by Gevers [1979], that weighted arithmetic averaging suffices for a consensual ordering.

9. SUBJECTIVE PROBABILITY

Before proceeding to the presentation of our method for finding a consensual probability assignment, we shall very briefly sketch the subjective or personalist method for finding probability assignments. Such subjective or personal probability assignments are a paradigm illustration of a quantitative summary of individual information. Once each individual provides a summary of his individual information in the form of a probability assignment to a set of hypotheses, we confront the problem of amalgamating or aggregating the individual assignments to find a consensual summary of the total information in the group. The method for finding subjective or personal probability assignments was originated by Ramsey [1931]. Ramsey notes that if there is some reward R that a person would prefer having rather than not having, and there is a repeatable event E such that a person is indifferent between the two gambles, G_1, such that the person receives R if E occurs and nothing if E does not occur, and G_2, such that the person receives R if E does not occur and nothing if E does occur, then the person, if he is rational, must assign a probability of .5 to E. The event E may be a flip of a normal coin turning up heads. From this starting point, other subjective or personal probabilities may be assigned by extrapolating from the preferences and indifferences of a person. Savage [1954] and Jeffrey [1965] have elaborated such a theory in systematic detail.

Perhaps the simplest way to understand the method is to assume that a person's subjective probabilities for games of chance, flipping coins or drawing cards from a deck, are what we would normally expect, though, in fact, such probabilities can be extracted from preferences and indifferences. We then consider how, starting with such probabilities, a person might confront the problem of assigning probabilities to hypotheses in a less structured domain, for example, to the hypothesis one has left a car unlocked. The method for finding the probability of the latter hypothesis, call it U, is to narrow the range in which it might fall. Suppose one thinks that U is highly probable but wonders whether it is more probable than 3/4. The hypothesis N affirming that a draw of a card from a standard deck would not be a heart is one to which one assigns a probability 3/4. Now let one consider the following two gambles. The first gamble, G_1, is such that one will receive $100 if N is true, and $0 if N is not true. The second gamble, G_2, is such that one will receive $100 if U is true, and $0 if U is not true.

Now imagine that one is offered a choice between the two gambles, and that one has the usual preference for receiving $100 as opposed to $0. Imagine also that the gamble would be paid off at the same time in either case by someone who knows, at that time, whether or not N and U are true. Suppose one prefers gamble G_1. Then one assigns a higher probability to N than U. For, assuming that one is rational, it would be reasonable for one to prefer G_1 to G_2 if and only if the probability of N is greater than the probability of U. If that is not obvious on intuitive grounds, then note that one's expectation on G_1 is the probability of N times \$100, while one's expectation on G_2 is the probability of U times \$100. Thus, N is more probable than U if and only if one's expectation on G_1 is greater than on G_2. If one is rational, one will prefer the gamble that offers one the greater expectation of gain. So, if one prefers G_1, one assigns a greater probability to N than to U and, therefore, assigns a probability less than 3/4 to U. If, on the other hand, one prefers gamble G_2, then one assigns a higher probability to U than to N, and, therefore, a higher probability than 3/4 to U. Finally, and most important, if one finds that one is indifferent between G_1 and G_2, then one assigns the same probability to N as to U and, therefore, a probability of 3/4 to U. When one is not indifferent, then more gambles must be compared before one can assign a probability to U.

It is important to note that the method, though it yields subjective or personal probability assignments, is intended to summarize information that may be perfectly objective. It may be based on precise measurement and statistical sampling. Perhaps the assignment of personal probabilities should be restrained by the limits of our objective information. For example, if our objective information tells us that the probability of a hypothesis must lie within a certain interval, the subjective probability must be assigned within that interval. It may not fall above the upper bound of the interval or beneath the lower bound. Predilections for such restraints depend on whether one believes that objective methods and probabilities must be ultimately extracted from subjective ones or *vice versa*.

Having noted that an individual can summarize information in terms of a probability assignment to a hypothesis, we note that individuals may be expected to disagree about the probability of an hypothesis when it is an interesting one concerning, for example, the biological determinants of human intelligence or social behavior. Even people on the same side of an issue could not be expected to assign exactly the same probability to the hypothesis in question. Once one gives precise articulation to the information one has, we should expect to find dissensus. The problem, then, is to find a mathematical method for aggregating the information thus articulated to determine what probability is the most reasonable to assign on the basis of the varying probabilities assigned by members of the group. Put another way, there will be some surface divergence, and the problem is to find a method for ascertaining a deeper level of consensus.

10. SUMMARY

Before developing our theory of consensual probability, it will be useful to provide a brief summary of our plan. In the next chapter, we shall present a theory of consensual probability. We present the theory as an algorithm or mechanical procedure for aggregating individual probability assignments. Our procedure involves, as a central feature, the computation of consensual weights assigned to each person on the basis of information people have about each other. The consensual probability assignment is a weighted arithmetic mean of the original probability assignments. In chapter 3, the same algorithm is applied to practical problems of social choice between alternatives. Here again consensual weights are computed from the information individuals possess about each other, but in this context the use of weighted arithmetic means is more controversial. Hence, we consider other methods for applying consensual weights in such contexts. In chapter 4, we consider an extension of our model for finding consensual weights permitting a realistic reevaluation of people by each other at different levels of evaluation. In chapter 5, we consider applications of our method in politics, ethics, science, and language. In chapter 6, we approach the matter axiomatically. Here we provide axioms that should be satisfied by any method for amalgamating individual assignments to obtain a consensus. In chapters 7 and 8, the mathematical foundations and consequences of our methodology are elaborated in detail.

Our theory will be justified by systematic articulation and application throughout the remainder of the book. Our initial justification for the method we shall present is that it is based on a fundamental precept of rationality to which people with different theoretical and practical preferences may subscribe. It is the precept to base decision on the available information. Our methodology is intended to achieve precisely the objective of aggregating information that individuals possess to reach consensus. It would be disingenuous, however, to attempt to conceal the fact that any procedure for aggregating information must be based on a special regimentation of the information and a rule of aggregation. Any regimentation of information gives us a summary and, therefore, some detail is sacrificed. Moreover, there will always be a multiplicity of logically possible methods for aggregating the information. We believe that our procedure for regimenting information does not require that any relevant information be ignored, though it is summarized in a special regimented form. We believe, as well, that our method of aggregation has obvious advantages, for example, that of cognitive and mathematical simplicity. Further defense of our methods will rest on the intuitive plausibility of articulation and the axiomatic development of conditions of adequacy. With these brief introductory remarks, we turn to the exposition of our theory.

CHAPTER TWO

THE ELEMENTARY METHOD AND
CONSENSUAL PROBABILITY

Our method for finding rational consensus rests on the fundamental assumption that members of a group have opinions about the dependability, reliability and rationality of other members of the group. Each member of the group is a source of information germane to deciding how much weight or respect should be given to the opinions or preferences of various members of the group. From this assumption we construct our model of rational consensus.

It will be useful to begin with a very simple model that will require subsequent modification. As a sample problem, suppose we have some relatively small group of members who know each other's opinion about some scientific question, for example, the question discussed by Dickie [1974] and Hill [1973] of whether the sun is round or oblate — and implications for Relativity Theory. Imagine that the group has engaged in extended discussion of the issue so that all empirical data and theoretical ratiocination has been communicated. Indeed, imagine the discussion has sufficiently exhausted the scientific information available so that further discussion would not change the opinion of any member of the group. We may call this a state of *dialectical equilibrium*. In this state, we suppose that each member has assigned some probability summarizing relevant information to the hypotheses, R, the sun is round, O, the sun is oblate, and, N, the sun is neither round nor oblate. Let $p_i^0(R)$ be the probability that i assigns to R in this initial or original state O. It should be expected that some dissensus or disagreement will prevail. Even if all in the group favored one hypothesis, it is unlikely that they would assign it the same probability.

1. ASSIGNMENT OF WEIGHTS

The problem is to find some probability assignment that constitutes the best summary of the total information in the group. It would be possible to sum the probabilities that members of the group assign to a given hypothesis, R say, and divide by the number of members. But the average probability would have one serious defect. It would give exactly equal weight to the probability assignment of each member of the group. Members of the group have not, however, committed themselves to such an average as a consensual probability. Moreover, there might be virtually unanimous agreement among members of the group that certain members of the group should be given more weight than others. In such a case, it would be all the more obvious that the simple average would not represent a consensual opinion of the group. The probability assignment of the least respected member would be given equal weight to the most respected in that average. If the most and least respected members assigned different probabilities to a hypothesis, the average might be too strongly influenced by the least respected of the group according to virtually all members of the group.

What is needed is some kind of average but an average that takes into consideration the weight or respect that members of group would assign to each other. Moreover, the average must be arrived at in such a way that all the members of the group are committed to such a probability assignment as a rational consensus. Suppose a given member of the group asks himself how much weight he would give to the opinions of each of the members of the group. To make the question more precise, let him ask how he would divide a unit vote among members of the group as potential selectors of an assignment for the group. There are a variety of methods a person might employ to decide how to divide the unit vote.

The choice of zero need not be arbitrary. To obtain a nonarbitrary zero, we suppose that the assignment of zero means that a person is worthless as a guide to selection. Thus, if the problem is to select a probability assignment for a hypothesis about the shape of the sun, the assignment of a value of zero to a person means that the person is worthless as a guide to the selection of a probability assignment for a hypothesis in solar astronomy. One way of ascertaining whether one regards another as worthless in this manner is to ask whether one would prefer following the guidance of the person in selecting a probability assignment for a hypothesis in some domain to a merely random selection of a probability assignment. If one does not prefer the person as a guide to truth over that a mere random mechanism, then the person should be assigned a value of zero. If one prefers that person as a guide over the random device, then some positive value should be assigned to the person. How a person might reasonably proceed to divide a unit vote among members of the group, himself included, depends on the particular problem under discussion and the sort of information the person has. For example, if members of the group have statistical information about past performance, weights might be assigned proportional to past successes and failures. Or, if members of the group have examined disjoint samples of a population, where the samples do not overlap in membership but do exhaust the population, then weights should be proportional to the size of the sample examined. In other cases, the assignment of weights will be reflective evaluations based on less regimented data.

We do not mandate any specific procedure in all cases. Other procedures will be discussed in chapter seven. We do require that the choice of the zero point be nonarbitrary so it is not relative to the membership of the group as would result if one simply assigned a value of zero to the least preferred selector in the group. For, such a selector, though the least preferred, might be either quite good or quite awful, and the resultant values would be unique only up to a positive linear transformation. If the choice of zero point is as in the method outlined, then the values have greater uniqueness as we intend that they should.

It may have occurred to a reader to wonder why a negative weight could not be assigned to a person. One answer is that a person cannot be worse than worthless as a guide to truth. Suppose a person is a perfectly reliable counter-inductive guide to the truth, however, in the sense that when the person assigns a probability of p to some hypothesis the opposite probability, $1 - p$, is the correct probability to be assigned. On a subjective probability assignment the notion of correctness is not perspicuous, but we allow treating the person as his mirror opposite and assigning a positive weight. To avoid problems arising with negative values, the person may be treated as though he assigned the value $1 - p$ and be assigned a positive weight.

2. WEIGHTED AGGREGATION

Now let us consider how such weights might be used. Suppose that person i surveys the probability assignments p_1^0, p_2^0, and so on to p_n^0 that members of the group assign to some hypothesis in an initial state. Person i notes that there is disagreement, that is, the probabilities differ. He may give great weight to his opinion, that is, the weight, w_{ii}, that i assigns to himself may be high or higher than the weight he assigns to any other member of the group, or he may give higher positive weight to others. The weights that he assigns to other members of the group summarize his information about their expertise and reliability. It is a measure that resembles a personal probability assignment. It is a numerical summary form of background knowledge that may include precise data about past success and more diffuse impressions of intellectual acuity.

Suppose every person gives some positive weight to the probability assignment of every other. It is reasonable for a person to accept the implications of the weights he assigns and attempt to improve upon his initial probability assignment by taking a weighted average, using the weights he assigns, of the probability assignments of members of the group. Person i would thus move from the initial state to a state one probability by the following summation:

$$p_i^1 = w_{i1}p_1^0 + w_{i2}p_2^0 + \ldots + w_{in}p_n^0.$$

Notice that there is a consistency argument in favor of such aggregation. If a person refuses to aggregate, though he does assign positive weight to other members, he is acting as though he assigned a weight of one to himself and a weight of zero to every other member of the group. If, in fact, he assigns positive weight to other members of the group, then he should not behave as though he assigned zero weight to them. We do not argue that no one should ever assign zero weight to the probability assignment of another. We only argue that *if* one assigns positive weight, one cannot consistently adopt a probability assignment that is equivalent to not giving any positive weight to that person. Moreover, since a person is allowed to assign himself a weight as well as others, he cannot complain that he is forced to neglect his own good opinion of himself by averaging in the manner indicated.

3. ITERATED AGGREGATION

Suppose, then, that each member of the group moves from his initial state probability, p_i^0, to his state one probability, p_i^1. Dissensus may be a feature of the state one probability assignments as well. If we allow that the state one probabilities are reasonable attempts to improve upon initial state probabilities, then we have a situation that is like the initial state, only each person has an improved probability assignment. This is the situation that person i confronts. Suppose the question arises as to what weight a person i should give to the state one probability assignments of other members of the group. Let us imagine, for the sake of simplicity, that member i assigns the same weight to each member of the group as he did initially. (We shall later consider changes in the weights assigned.) There is the same argument for aggregation in state one as in the initial state. Person i may attempt to improve his probability assignment by taking a weighted average of the state one probability assignments to arrive at a state two probability as follows: $p_i^2 = w_{i1}p_1^1 + w_{i2}p_2^1 + \ldots + w_{in}p_n^1$. The argument for averaging is again one of consistency. If the person refuses to aggregate, that is equivalent to assigning others a weight of zero and aggregating. Since, in fact, he does not assign them a weight of zero, his refusal to average is inconsistent with the weights that he actually assigns.

Suppose that each person in the group, discerning the compelling force of the reasoning just given, moves from state one to state two. It is apparent that this argument may be cogently reiterated as long as there is dissensus about the probabilities in question. Therefore, the process should be continued as long as dissensus prevails. Given the assumptions we have made, this process converges toward a consensual probability assignment, p_c, for all members of the group. There is no proof that reiterated aggregation will reach a stage at which every one will adopt the consensual probability, p_c, but assignments of members of the group will converge toward that as the limit in an infinite sequence of aggregation. This is a consequence of the assumptions that we have made, though, as we shall note, a weaker set of assumptions is sufficient to guarantee the convergence.

The assumptions that we have made are (i) the positive respect condition, which says that every member of the group assigns a positive weight to every member of the group, (ii) the constancy condition, which says that every member of the group remains constant at every stage in the weight that he assigns to a specific member of the group, and (iii) the aggregation condition, which says each member of the group takes a weighted average of the probability assignments of members of the group at each stage to improve upon his probability assignment.

We must qualify our claim that aggregation is a reasonable method for improving a probability assignment. This is a normative claim about rationality. There is no presumption that such aggregation leads to some "objectively" correct probability assignment. The justification for aggregation is that it amalgamates the information available within the group in a rational manner. One might object to this claim either on the grounds that the weights are not an adequate representation of information or that the weights could be used in some other way, to average in some other manner, for example. We have already replied to the first objection. We shall offer an axiomatic defense of arithmetical averaging in Chapter 6. A brief defense of arithmetic averaging is that other forms of averaging considered in later chapters would not guarantee that the aggregator would obtain a probability assignment that satisfies the calculus of probability when his original assignment does.

4. MATHEMATICS OF CONSENSUS

With these qualifications noted, let us examine the mathematical structure of our argument. If we consider the aggregation as a process of the entire group, what takes place is that a matrix of weights is multiplied by a column of probabilities. Consider the following:

$$W = \begin{bmatrix} w_{11} & w_{12} & \cdots & w_{1n} \\ w_{21} & w_{22} & \cdots & w_{2n} \\ \cdots & \cdots & \cdots & \cdots \\ w_{n1} & w_{n2} & \cdots & w_{nn} \end{bmatrix} \qquad P = \begin{bmatrix} p_1^0 \\ p_2^0 \\ \cdot \cdot \\ p_n^0 \end{bmatrix}$$

The matrix W is the table of weights, and P is a column of probabilities assigned in the initial state. The transition from the initial state to state one consists of finding the product WP. The matrix is multiplied by the column to obtain a new column so that p_i^1 is the sum of the products $w_{ij}p_j^0$. Thus, WP is the column of state one probabilities. To move to state two, then, we take the product of W and WP, $W(WP)$, or W^2P. State three is W^3P, and state n is W^nP. Thus, as n goes to infinity, we get convergence toward a column of probabilities in which each probability in the column is the consensual probability, p_c.

The process by which we arrive at the consensual probability, p_c, is thus mathematically equivalent to one in which we aggregate weights until we arrive at a consensual weight w_i for each member of the group and then find the consensual probability, p_c, by summing the products $w_ip_i^0$. As the power of the matrix W is raised, we converge toward a matrix in which every person assigns the same weight, the consensual weight, w_i, to a given person i. Different people may receive different consensual weights. The matrix multiplication converges toward a matrix with every row the same, though the columns pay differ. The convergent set of weights multiplied by the original column P is the sum of the products $w_ip_i^0$, the consensual weights multiplied by the original probability assignments. Thus, the aggregation by which we proceed from the initial probability assignment to a consensual probability assignment is equivalent to one in which we ignore the probability assignment, proceed to find consensual weight assignments, and calculate the consensual probability assignment as a weighted average of the original probability assignment.

We can give an alternative account of the process of finding consensual probabilities by first finding consensual weights. Suppose that each person has assigned an initial weight to all members of the group. Consider the position of person i at this stage. Let the original weight that a person i assigns to j be w_{ij}^0. Person i then notes that the weights that members of the group assign to a person j differ, that is, w_{1j}^0, w_{2j}^0, and so on are not all the same. Person i might then attempt to improve on the weight that he has assigned to person j by amalgamating the information members of the group summarize in the weights they assign to j. Person i could, of course, simply take the average of the weights members of the group assign to j, but that would not be the most reasonable way to proceed. For, person i has differential information about members of the group. He may not think that all are equally good evaluators. To use all the information he has at this stage, it is reasonable for him to attempt to improve upon the weight that he assigns to person j by taking a weighted average of the weights that members assign to j. Thus, person i might move from his original weight, w_{ij}^0, to an improved state one weight, w_{ij}^1, by taking the sum of the products $w_{ix}^0 w_{xj}^0$ for every value of x, that is, for every member of the group from 1 to n. If person i does this for each member of the group, then he will obtain an improved row of weights, w_{i1}^1, w_{i2}^1 and so on. If each member of the group does this, each person in the group will obtain a new row of weights. The result will be a new matrix which is WW or W^2. This form of aggregation is the multiplication of the matrix W by a matrix, in this case the same matrix W.

Of course, dissensus might prevail in state one. Person i might then again consider how to improve his assignment of a weight to person j. One way he might proceed is to take the weighted average of the state one weights people assign to j, using his original weights to find the average. He would take the sum of the products $w_{ix}^0 w_{xj}^1$ to find an improved weight for j. If all people in the group proceed in this way, we obtain the result of multiplying W by W^2 and obtain W^3. This would not be the most reasonable way for person i to proceed, however. Since he has obtained w_{ix}^1 as an improved weight to assign to x, it is more reasonable for him to use the improved weight to further improve the weight he assigns to j rather than retrogressing to the original weights. So, his improved weight for j would be the sum of the products $w_{ix}^1 w_{xj}^1$. If everyone proceeds in this way, the result is that of multiplying W^2 by W^2 to obtain W^4. This process is one that may be expected to converge more rapidly towards consensus than the process of iterated aggregation of probabilities first presented, but convergence will be toward the same consensual weights. The consensual probability reached by iterated aggregation of the probabilities from stage to stage will be the same as the consensual probability reached by iterated aggregation of weights converging toward consensual weights then used to compute the consensual probability as the consensual weighted average of the original probabilities.

It must be noted that special constraints are needed to insure that a consensual probability assignment satisfies the calculus of probability. Put in terms of the second method, the same consensual weights must be used to find consensual probabilities for a set of pairwise disjoint and mutually exhaustive statements. Consensual probabilities of disjunctions of such statements may then be computed by addition, and statements logically equivalent to such disjunctions or to the original statements must be assigned the same values. These constraints will insure that consensual probability assignments satisfy the calculus of probability if the original individual probability assignments do so.

It is important to notice that in our normative model the process of aggregating should be thought of as a heuristic fiction. Mathematically, the original weight matrix determines a Markov chain familiar to physicists. Applications of Markov chains to find empirical consensus were proposed by Harary [1959] and French [1956]. DeGroot [1974] proposed using Markov chains to reach consensus and proposed that his methodology be regarded as a formalization of the Delphi method of, for example, Helmer [1963]. Our use of the mathematics is, like DeGroot's, a normative model. The model may have some value as an empirical idealization. We shall consider such an interpretation of the model subsequently. But the process is not essential in the normative interpretation. It is only the convergent values that matter. The mathematical method shows us how to arrive at consensual weights or consensual probabilities from the initial stage. The mathematics serves to extract the consequences of rational evaluation in the initial state. Thus the model is a synchronic rather than a dynamic model of rationality. It tells us what the total information contained in the group in the initial state adds up to at a specific stage of information acquisition.

5. ZERO RESPECT

The restriction that positive weights be assigned to all members of the group by every member of the group is unrealistic. The assumption of universal positive respect yields convergence in the aggregation process, but it is by no means a necessary condition. Some member of the group might wish to give no weight to the probability assigned by some members of the group. If person i assigns zero weight to some member of the group, that means that person i believes the probability assignment of the person in question is worthless and should be completely discounted. It is possible, moreover, that person i might assign a weight of zero to someone he does not know at all. Not knowing the person in question, person i might decide to follow a policy of maximal caution and assume the worst. The example we have imagined in our exposition is one in which a group is in contact and has discussed some subject to the point of dialectical equilibrium. We shall wish to broaden the application of the model to groups that have not fulfilled this condition. One may wish to provide a summary of the information groups possess when members have not exhaustively discussed a subject and are not in such complete personal contact or interaction. Members of such a group may assign a weight of zero to some other members.

The question arises of how many zeroes members can assign to other members of the group before convergence is destroyed. The answer, rather surprisingly, is that if some member assigns a positive weight to himself, then convergence may be obtained from each person assigning positive weight to only one other person, provided the pattern of positive respect connects the members appropriately. For example, if each member of the group communicates positive respect to every other member of the group through intermediaries, then convergence will result. Let us say that there is a chain of positive respect from i to j in the group if and only if there is a sequence of members of the group with i as the first member of the sequence and j as the last such that each member of the group assigns positive weight to the next member in the sequence. Convergence toward positive consensual weights results from iterated aggregation if there is a chain of positive respect from each member of the group to every other member of the group, and at least one member assigns positive weight to himself. We call this communication of respect.

We might imagine cases in which no member assigns positive weight to themselves, perhaps because they are prohibited from doing so. A method for finding consensual weights in such cases will be examined in detail in Chapter Seven. We note here that if no member assigns positive weight to himself but there is a chain of positive respect from every other member to every other member of the group, then if we specify a positive standard weight less than unity for each member to assign to himself, reducing the weights that he assigns to others proportionately so that the weights a person assigns sum to unity, we will obtain convergence. Moreover, the same consensual weights and probabilities result no matter what positive standard weight is chosen provided it is less than unity. What will determine the convergent or consensual weights is the proportional assignment of weights to others. Thus, if we were to modify the model disallowing members of the group to assign weights to themselves, and stipulating instead some positive standard weight less than unity that each must assign to himself, the standard weight could be arbitrarily chosen without affecting the consensus.

6. NUMERICAL ILLUSTRATION

It may be useful to have some numerical illustrations of our model to consider the consequences that result from the initial assignment of weights. Let us first consider a very simple distribution of weights:

.8	.2	0	0	0	0
0	.7	.3	0	0	0
0	0	.6	.4	0	0
0	0	0	.6	.4	0
0	0	0	0	.7	.3
.2	0	0	0	0	.8

Here each person gives positive respect to only one other person, the next person in the group, and the resulting consensual weights are:

$$.23 \quad .15 \quad .12 \quad .12 \quad .15 \quad .23^1$$

If each person in the group evenly distributes the weight he is willing to give to others instead of simply assigning it to the next person in the group, the resulting convergence will be the same though it will occur more rapidly.

However, if all the members of the group assign weights as in the original example except for the first person who splits the weight he gives to others between the next two members as follows:

$$8. \quad .1 \quad .1 \quad 0 \quad 0 \quad 0$$

then the consensus is:

$$.25 \quad .08 \quad .13 \quad .13 \quad .17 \quad .25.$$

The effect is to slightly raise the consensual values of the two most self-confident members, but the member originally respected by the first member loses weight as a result of his dividing his respect between two.

If we imagine that the third and fifth members also change their assignments, splitting the positive weight they give to others unevenly, we might get the following matrix:

8.	.1	.1	0	0	0
0	.7	.3	0	0	0
0	0	.6	.3	.1	0
0	0	0	.6	.4	0
.1	0	0	0	.7	.2
.2	0	0	0	0	.8

The consensus is:

$$.28 \quad .09 \quad .14 \quad .11 \quad .19 \quad .19.$$

Here the assignment of positive weight by the third person to the fifth raised his consensual weight, and the assignment of positive weight by the fifth person to the first person raised his consensual weight. The fourth and sixth persons lose in the consensual assignment because less weight is assigned to them. The first person gains, and some of his gain is received by the second and third persons to whom he assigns positive weight.

7. COMBINED GROUPS

Another interesting illustration arises when we have two groups of people, each group containing a member who gives himself a high weight that is not discounted by other members of the group, and the two groups are linked by some, perhaps small, positive respect. Thus, suppose we consider the following matrix:

$$
\begin{array}{cccccc}
.5 & .49 & .009 & 0 & 0 & .001 \\
.05 & .9 & .05 & 0 & 0 & 0 \\
.009 & .49 & .5 & .001 & 0 & 0 \\
0 & 0 & .001 & .5 & .49 & .009 \\
0 & 0 & 0 & .050 & .9 & .050 \\
.001 & 0 & 0 & .009 & .49 & .5
\end{array}
$$

The upper left quandrant and the lower right quandrant contain the two groups with communication of respect between them effected by the first, third, fourth and sixth members. The second and fifth members of the larger group give much higher weight to themselves than they give to others, and they assign zero weight to each other. The limit is:

$$.042 \quad .415 \quad .042 \quad .042 \quad .415 \quad 0.42$$

The second and fifth members give only one tenth as much weight to others as others give them, and, as a result, they receive ten times as much consensual weight as others. We shall discuss this matrix and variations of it in some detail, and we shall refer to it as the *standard* matrix.

If the second member of the group assigns a somewhat lower weight to himself, for example, if he assigns twice as much weight to members one and three as in the standard matrix so that his weight vector is

$$.1 \quad .8 \quad .1 \quad 0 \quad 0 \quad 0$$

he will receive only half as much consensual weight as member five, the other highly weighted member, and the convergence will be as follows:

.053   .262   .053   .053   .524   .053.

The lower weighted members of the group increase in weight somewhat from the doubling of weight assigned by the second member to the first and third, in fact, each of the lower weighted members increase in the consensus by one quarter. Similar proportional increases occur when the second person again doubles the weight assigned to the first and third persons so he has the weight vector

.2   .6   .2   0   0   0

and the consensus is:

.062   .151   .062   .062   .603   .062.

One might wonder what the consequence would result if members of one group give respect to different members of the other group. If the assignment is symmetrical, the convergence is the same as in the standard matrix. For example, if the first and third members assign .001 to the fifth person instead of to the sixth and fourth persons respectively, while the fourth and sixth persons assign .001 to the second person instead of third and first persons respectively, the consensual values are the same as for the standard matrix. Moreover, even if the first and third persons make this reassignment and the fourth and sixth persons remain as in the standard matrix, the same consensus will also result. However, one should not conclude from this that it is only the total weight communicated from one group to the other that matters. For example, if the second person assigns .002 to the fifth person, instead of the first and third persons assigning .001 to the sixth and fourth persons respectively, the outcome is radically altered. The matrix would be

.5	.49	.01	0	0	0
.049	.9	.049	0	.002	0
.010	.49	.5	0	0	0

in the first three rows and the same as the standard matrix in the next three. The consensus is:

.008   .077   .008   .077   .754   .077

and here the second person receives only one tenth the weight received by the fifth person. Even if the second person only assigns .001 to the fifth person, the first and third remaining as just indicated, so the second person has the vector

.0495   .9   .0495   0   .001   0

the consensus strongly favoring the fifth person is:

.014   .141   .014   .07   .69   .07

and here the fifth person has five times the weight of the second.

On the other hand, if both the heavily weighted members, two and five, each assign the same amount to some member of the other group, say .001, then the result is the same as the standard matrix. For example, the following matrix has that result:

.5	.49	.01	0	0	0
.0495	.9	.0495	0	.001	0
.01	.49	.5	0	0	0
0	0	0	.5	.49	.01
.001	0	0	.0495	.9	.0495
0	0	0	.01	.49	.5

When person five doubles the weight he assigns to person one and so has the vector

.002   0   0   .049   .9   .049

the consensual weight assigned to person two is twice as large as that assigned to person five as follows:

.057   .554   .056   .028   .277   .028.

Here the first and third persons also receive twice as much weight as the fourth and sixth persons. The nature of the proportional shifts is obvious.

Let us now return to the standard matrix with a modification in the second row assigning much higher weight to the first member by the second as follows:

.15   .8   .05   0   0   0

from which we obtain the following consensus:

.079   .262   .028   .053   .524   .054.

The first person receives higher weight, but in the standard matrix the first person assigns a weight of .001 to the six person and, indirectly, to the second group. As a result, the fifth person, who is heavily weighted in the second group, receives twice as much weight in the convergence as the second person. If the first person shifts more weight to the second group by assigning .1 to the fifth person, the convergent shift is yet more radical. Thus if person one has the vector

$$.5 \quad .39 \quad .009 \quad 0 \quad .1 \quad .001$$

and the second person is as above, the consensus is:

$$.002 \quad .014 \quad .002 \quad .083 \quad .816 \quad .083.$$

This is, of course, a dramatic shift of weight, but when one notices that person one has assigned one hundred times more weight to a member of the second group than originally, the result is not so surprising.

One final variation on the standard matrix occurs when the second person assigns a weight of .15 to the first person as in the previous paragraph, but the first person does not assign any weight to members of the other group. If the third member assigns .002 to the fourth member so that the sum assigned by each group to the other is .002, we obtain a matrix that differs from the standard matrix in the first three rows as follows:

$$
\begin{array}{cccccc}
.5 & .49 & .01 & 0 & 0 & 0 \\
.15 & .8 & .05 & 0 & 0 & 0 \\
.008 & .49 & .5 & .002 & 0 & 0
\end{array}
$$

and the consensus is:

$$.113 \quad .376 \quad .040 \quad .040 \quad .391 \quad .040.$$

It is clear here that this strategy paid off for the first person. As a result of not assigning weight to the other group, he retains the weight assigned to him by person two rather passing on the benefit of that weight to the second group. These results illustrate how the effects of shifting of individual weights influence the consensual weights received by others.

8. RADICAL CHANGE

The model also gives us one account of radical change in science, such as that discussed by Kuhn [1962], when a new consensual probability assignment emerges from the combination of two previously unlinked groups resulting from an increase of respect among members of the two groups. Thus, suppose that there are two groups discussing some issue but that the two groups do not have a combined consensual probability assignment because the groups do not respect each other. The members of each of the groups do communicate respect within the group. So at the initial time, t, there are two consensual probability assignments, p_{c1}, for group number one, and p_{c2}, for group number two. It may happen that group number one assigns a very high probability to some hypothesis H to which group number two assigns a very low probability. Suppose the first group is the standard bearer for the most widely accepted theory in a field. The second group is one that favors an alternative theory and assigns a much lower probability to the commonly advocated theory. Imagine, moreover, that no new evidence germane to the evaluation of the standard theory and the alternative theory develops from the time t to some later time t'. What happens during the interval from t to t', however, is that members of two groups communicate, directly or through the periodical literature in the field, and respect is increased as a result of the interchange. Hence, at time t', the two groups collectively compose a combined group in which respect is communicated. There will be at t' a consensual probability assignment p_{c3} for the combined group that did not exist at t. It may be the case that the consensual probability assignment of the combined group coincides with the consensual probability assignment of the second group at time t, or is very close to that value. In that case, the larger consensus will favor the alternative theory.

If we view this process from the standpoint of a member of the first group, which favored the standard theory at t, the result might seem capricious and irrational. For, at t, they have a consensus that H is highly probable, and, though there is another group that disagrees with them, they discount that group. No weight is given to the consensus of that group. At time t', a radical shift has occurred. The first group is absorbed into a larger group, and the consensus in this group assigns H a low probability. They are consensually committed to a probability widely at variance with the original probability representing their consensus at time t. Since no new experimental evidence has been found in the interval, the shift in probability that has occurred may seem unwarranted. Actually, however, the shift is justified by the aggregation of a wider base of information in the composite group.

Such shifts may motivate historians and sociologists of science to describe scientific changes as resulting form social influence rather than from empirical information. Of course, shifts that actually occur may well be influenced by a diversity of factors. If, however, consensus represents an aggregation of information contained in a group, an amalgamation of the total information of truth seekers summarized in probabilities and weights, then the consensus conforms to a central canon of scientific methodology. The principle is that it is irrational to ignore relevant evidence and rational to do the opposite. The common opinion of a group may be formed by nonscientific considerations, but when it coincides with the consensus that would result from the rational aggregation of total information in the group, it is, with the qualifications mentioned above, a rational guide to scientific truth.

9. ILLUSTRATION OF RADICAL CHANGE

Joining two groups can be shocking for a member of a group that is swamped by the consensus of a larger group. This is most dramatically represented when one individual respects and is respected by a member of another group, and it is this reciprocation that communicates respect in the larger group. Consider, for example, the following group of three:

.900	.100	0
0	.950	.05
.014	0	.986

A row is the weights assigned by one member of the group to the members of the group. The consensual weights for the group would be as follows:

.100	.200	.700

Thus, the third person in the group receives great weight, and the consensual probability for the group would be close to his personal probability.

Now consider what would happen if this group were linked to another group of three as a result of the first member of this group assigning a small weight of .001 to the member of another group who reciprocates by assigning the same weight to him establishing communication of respect between the two groups. We then have the following matrix in which the original group of three is contained in the lower right hand quadrant with the modification mentioned:

.900	.100	0	0	0	0
0	.950	.050	0	0	0
.013	0	.986	.001	0	0
0	0	.001	.900	.099	0
0	0	0	0	.950	.050
0	0	0	.014	0	.986

In this instance, the other group, represented by the upper left hand quadrant, has a similar internal structure of weights. The converging consensus is as follows:

.048   .097   .367   .051   .099   .388.

Since the consensual weight for the third person in the original group, who is the sixth person in this larger group, is .338, he has already lost considerable influence upon the consensual probability assignment as a result of the first member of his group giving some small weight to a reciprocating member of another group. Notice the second person in the group who assigns positive weight to the third member does not alter his assignment. So the third member will find that, though the direct respect he received for his expertise is the same as before, the consensus has slipped away from him. The consensual probability assignment for the larger group may not be as close to his as to that of his rival in the other group who receives a higher consensual weight of .367.

Moreover, if the first member of the second group gives a slightly greater weight to the member of the other group he respects, the results can be even more striking. Suppose, for example, that we have the same matrix as above except that the third person receives a weight of .010 instead of .001 from the fourth person and the fourth row is as follows:

0   0   .010   .900   .09   0

In that case, the consensual weight assignment is:

.054   .108   .424   .046   .082   .286

Here the sixth person has lost more influence, having now only a consensual weight of .286 instead of .700 as he had in the original three person group. Yet the amount of direct respect he receives is the same.

Of course, things can get much worse for the sixth person. For example, suppose the third person raises the weight he assigns the fourth person to .010, perhaps reciprocating that weight assigned to him by the fourth person. The fourth person, however, is even more respectful of the third and raises the weight he assigns to that person to .099. We then obtain the original matrix altered so that the third row is

.004   0   .986   .010   0   0

and the fourth row is

0   0   .099   .900   .001   0.

In this case the consensual weights for the group are

$$.033 \quad .065 \quad .813 \quad .082 \quad .002 \quad .006.$$

The result is obvious. The sixth person is reduced to but a shadow of his former self, his consensual weight having been reduced from .700 to .006. The sixth person gives positive weight to the fourth person who assigns no positive weight to him. This may further reinforce the feeling of the sixth person that the resulting consensus, which will be dominated by the third person, is catastrophic. From his personal point of view, that may be so. But, if the weights represent the best summary of information the members can provide, the resulting consensus is a rational aggregation of the total information. Anticipation of such consequences may, however, explain why an individual could prefer to be an iconoclast who refuses to give any positive weight to others.

10. SUMMARY AND PROSPECTUS

We have proposed in this chapter an elementary model of rational consensus. The advantage of the model is that it aggregates the information in a group articulated as probabilities and weights, and, therefore, the consensus obtained is a summary of that information. We note that whether someone is committed to the consensus will depend on whether he is committed to the procedure of aggregation. In Chapter 5, we shall present an extended model for finding rational consensus that is more sophisticated than the elementary model methodologically and, therefore, permits us to argue more effectively for the conclusion that members of a group communicating respect are committed to the consensual outcome. In the extended model, we eliminate the need for the constancy condition, where the same weights are assigned at each level, and explain why such constancy should not be expected. The explanation is that weights assigned at different levels express different information. We shall also propose a method for assigning weights at each level that is superior to the method of simply discoursing until a group reaches a state of dialectical equilibrium. The method separates the information articulated at each level of weighting. Consequently, we obtain a cogent argument for aggregating at each level, namely, that new information is amalgamated. The extended model is the one we ultimately wish to defend, and the elementary model is merely a simplified approximation to it. Before turning to the complications of the extended model, however, we shall exploit the simplicity of the elementary model in application to the domain of practical decision making and social choice.

NOTE

[1] The numerical examples are rounded off values obtained by Mark Lehrer from computer simultation.

CHAPTER THREE

THE ELEMENTARY METHOD AND SOCIAL CHOICE

We shall now examine the application of the elementary model to questions of practical decision and social choice. In such cases, a rational choice between alternatives is sought, and information from individuals about those alternatives is amalgamated. The information from individuals might not be numerical, however, but rather a ranking of alternatives articulating individual preferences. Moreover, even when there is numerical information, expressed in terms of a utility function for example, there may be reasons against aggregating or using a weighted average to make the choice. The utility assignments of individuals may fail to satisfy necessary conditions of rigidity. We shall discuss such conditions in detail in Chapter 6 below and later in the present chapter. It will be noted that our approach is indebted to Arrow [1951], [1977], in that we regard the output of social choice as the ordering of a set of alternatives. We advocate the use of information beyond individual profiles of preferences, namely, the weights individuals assign to each other at various levels for obtaining the consensual ordering when such information is applicable.

1. WEIGHTS AND SOCIAL CHOICE

We shall first approach the problem of social choice by examining the application of consensual weights to situations in which alternatives are not evaluated numerically, and we shall proceed to cases in which they are. By so doing, we presuppose, at first, only a preference ordering of alternatives and use information concerning consensual weights to obtain the consensual ordering. We note again that when the aggregation procedure is applied to some numerically scored allocation problem, the resulting process is mathematically equivalent to one in which consensual weights are first found and then used for a single averaging of the values to be allocated.

Let us consider an example of practical decision making involving a social group. Suppose we confront some issue of choice within a small group, for example a question about what form of therapy to use in the treatment of a patient. In this country, such a decision is unlikely to be made by a group, but in other countries, China for example, the decision might well be made by committee, one involving not only doctors and nurses but even nonmedical personnel. It is possible that such a decision would be made by a group in this country as well, one involving more than one member of the medical profession and, perhaps, members of the patient's family as well. Moreover, even if a single individual, the doctor or the patient, is to make the decision, they might wish to obtain the advice of others and to determine what consensus would be rational for the group.

Let us consider a medical example, one in which the patient has cancer for example, and the decision is what form of therapy, surgery, radiology, chemeotherapy or combination of these should be applied. If there is a difference of opinion after extended discussion and a decision must be made, whether by the committee or by some individual, it would be relevant to determine how much weight it is reasonable to give to each member of the group. As in the previous chapter, each individual assigns a weight to every member of the group by dividing a unit vote thus obtaining initial state weights. Let the weight that individual i assigns to j in the initial state be w_{ij}^0. The individual i then considers the weights that each member of the group assigns to j in the initial state. With the objective of improving upon the weight that he assigns to j, the individual i might take a weighted average of weights that members assign to j, using the initial weight assigned to a person to average the weight that the person assigns to j. Thus, the improved weight w_{ij}^1 person i assigns to j in state one is the sum $w_{i1}^0 w_{1j}^0 + w_{i2}^0 w_{2j}^0$ and so forth to $w_{in}^0 w_{nj}^0$. Individual i might then consider the various weights that members of the group assign to person j in state one and attempt to improve further upon the weight assigned to j. Individual i takes a weighted average of the state one weights assigned to j, using this time his state one weights to average the weight that each person assigns to j. This aggregation is obtained by adding one to the superscripts in the summation formula above. If there is communication of respect in the group, continued aggregation will converge toward a positive consensual weight for each person in the group. There will be a set of consensual weights w_1, w_2 and so forth to w_n summarizing all the information contained in the group about the reliability of members of the group.

The mathematical results are the same as in the probability case. It is important to notice, however, that if the individuals are to be rationally committed to the consensus, the weights assigned must be *rationally* assigned. If the consensual weights represent bias, that is, if every person evaluates others simply in terms of how closely they agree with him, then there is little reason for a person to feel committed to the resulting consensus. A similar reservation would apply if an individual were convinced that the members of the group were totally ignorant of each others expertise or were too blinded by prejudice to evaluate each other rationally. However, if the weights each person assigns to others are informed and disinterested, in that manner rational, then they represent an aggregation of total information. They constitute a rational summary of information in the group. The consensus results from the rational opinions of members of the group. Thus, the evaluations expressed in weights must be rational. A weight that individual i assigns to j is his comparative evaluation of j among members of the group as a judge of what the best decision or choice would be from among a specific set of alternatives. If there is a chain of positive respect from every member of the group to every other member of the group, then the group communicates respect. Such a group is an ethical community. When a group fails to communicate respect, it decomposes into ethical subcommunities. When the subcommunities consist of single members only, then ethical anarchy prevails.

With these reflections before us, let us consider the various ways in which consensual weights might be used to make some choice or decision. The ideal case in dialectical equilibrium is one in which the group communicates respect. This allows us to find a summary of the total information germane to social choice that members of the group have about each other. To distinguish this information from the more direct information members of the group have about the subject matter of the choice, medical information for example, we shall refer to the consensual weights as a summary of social information. Let us consider any group for which there is a set of consensual weights. We have then a summary of the social information. How should we use this information in making a social choice?

2. WEIGHTED DICTATORSHIP

The person given the highest consensual weight might be selected to dictate the social choice of the alternative that is his rational preference. This method of weighted dictatorship raises the problem of how to proceed when several members of the group are assigned the same maximal consensual weight. Two procedures are available in the case of ties. One is to select by lottery one of those assigned the top weight to dictate the social choice. This strategy will, however, seem unreasonable when a large majority of those assigned the top weight prefer the same alternative. It will then seem that the majority should rule. The first method, whether articulated in such a way that ties are resolved by lottery or by majority of those at the top, is an unrefined use of the social information available. In addition to information about who receives the top consensual weight, we should also exploit the information about other members of the group. This would be especially evident in the case in which the difference between the highest consensual weight and all others was miniscule. A more refined use of social information would be to use the weights in such a way that the weight assigned to a person represents his chance of being selected to dictate the social choice. This could be accomplished with a lottery in which the chance of being selected is directly proportional to the consensual weight assigned. One person is chosen by lottery to dictate the social choice.

3. UTILITIES FROM WEIGHTS

There is a method for using the consensual weights that is a more sophisticated exploitation of social information. Instead of using the weights to choose someone to dictate the social choice, they may be used to construct a social utility function. The method is to let $u_s(A_i)$, the social utility of A_i, be the sum of weights of all those members for whom A_i is the first preference. When some member i has k alternatives ranked first, then w_i/k is assigned to each of those alternatives for the summation.

4. UTILITIES AND LOWER LEVEL PREFERENCES

In spite of the advantages of this method, however, it has the defect of ignoring information about lower level preferences. Consider, for example, the case in which there is very little agreement about first preferences but total unanimity about second preferences. The unanimous second preference of everyone in the group would, by the method, be assigned a social utility of 0, while the first preference of a single person would be assigned a social utility equal to his consensual weight. Though providing us with a finer grained method for using social information than the preceding methods, it filters out important information concerning preferences among alternatives.

Methods sensitive to information about all preferences, as well as to social information expressed in the consensual weights, is available. Instead of computing a social utility function by taking the sum of the weights of first preferences alone, we take a sum that reflects the preference ordering of each individual. More specifically, where w_i is the consensual weight assigned to i, we assign a measure m_i to the preferences of i as follows: $m_i(A_j) = w_i/r$, where r is the rank assigned to A_j, the top rank being 1, the second 2 and so forth. That formula is adequate assuming that there are no ties. If n options are tied at rank r, then the m_i value for an option at that rank is $w_i/r + w_i/r+1 + w_i/r+2 + \ldots + w_i/r + (n-1)$ divided by n. The social utility function for an option A_j is then the sum of the m values assigned to A_j by members of the group. If all the members of the group agreed on a second choice, everybody's second choice might have the highest social utility.

This method exploits the rank ordering of the information contained in the preference ranking and weighting. However, an arbitrary element is introduced. The difference between the value of a first and second choice is greater than the difference between a second and third choice, and the difference between a second and third choice is greater than the difference between a third and fourth choice, and so on. Whether this is desirable or unacceptable will depend on the emphasis one thinks it is appropriate to give to higher preferences. One could, of course, calculate the social utility function in terms of a measure other than m and avoid this consequence. For example, measure m^* would accomplish this objective where $m^*_i(A_j) = sw_i$, where s is equal to n if A_j is top ranked, s is equal to $(n-1)$ if A_j is ranked second, and s is equal to $(n-(r-1))$ if A_j is ranked r. Ties would create an additional complication. The arbitrariness of the choice of these measure functions indicates an underlying inadequacy in the approach. Whatever method we use for the construction of a measure function will introduce an arbitrary method for deciding how strongly a person prefers his first choice over his second, his second over this third, and so forth.

5. WEIGHTED UTILITIES

This consideration leads us directly to a method that, when applicable, should be preferred. It is the method of *weighted utilities*. To simplify our representation, let the utility that individual i assigns to alternative j be represented by a_{ij}. Thus, individual i will have utility values a_{i1}, a_{i2}, and so forth to a_{ik} for the pairwise disjoint and mutually exhaustive set of alternatives A_1, A_2, and so forth to A_k. The result is that we have a vector of consensual weights and a matrix of individual utility values as follows:

$$C = [w_1 \quad w_2 \quad \ldots \quad w_n] \qquad A = \begin{bmatrix} a_{11} & a_{12} & \ldots & a_{1k} \\ a_{21} & a_{22} & \ldots & a_{2k} \\ \ldots & \ldots & \ldots & \ldots \\ a_{n1} & a_{n2} & \ldots & a_{nk} \end{bmatrix}$$

Assuming C is the vector of consensual weights for the n members of the group, we obtain the weighted average or consensual utility assignment for each alternative by CA.

6. CONSENSUS THROUGH AGGREGATION

Once it is assumed that we have a utility assignment for each individual, the consensual utility assignment may be reached by the same method as the consensual probability assignments. Obtaining a consensual utility assignment using consensual weights to compute the weighted average of individual utility assignments is mathematically equivalent to a process whereby individuals use the original weights that they assign to members of the group to improve their individual utility assignments by iteratered weighted averaging of individual utilities. Thus, suppose individual i assigns a utility a_{ij}^0 to alternative j originally, that is, in the initial state, and asks himself how reliable members of the group are as a guide to how good the various alternatives are, dividing a unit vote among the n members of the group to articulate his answer. He might then improve upon his initial state utility and obtain a state one utility assignment by taking a weighted average of the utility assignments of members of the group obtaining state one utility a_{ij}^1 from the aggregation $w_{i1}a_{1j}^0 + w_{i2}a_{2j}^0 + \ldots + w_{in}a_{nj}^0$. One justification for this aggregation is consistency, since refusing to aggregate is equivalent to assigning everyone else a weight of zero and aggregating. The other justification is that aggregation utilizes the social information the individual has about the reliability of members of the group.

Once members of the group have aggregated to obtain their state one utility assignments for the group, they may again note some differences, and, for the same reason, aggregate again, this time aggregating the state one utility assignments. This amounts to simply adding 1 to the superscripts in the formula above. If differences remain in state one, they may proceed to state two by again adding one to the superscripts in the formula, and so on from stage to stage. The argument for iterated aggregation is again consistency and the utilization of social information. According to the elementary model, which we shall modify in the next chapter, the weights remain constant from stage to stage. Given communication of respect, the process of iteration will converge toward a set of consensual utilities for the alternatives in question. These consensual utilities will be the same as those arrived at by taking the weighted average of the original utilities using consensual weights.

Mathematically the process just described is one in which the matrix

$$W = \begin{bmatrix} w_{11} & w_{12} & \cdots & w_{1n} \\ w_{21} & w_{22} & \cdots & w_{2n} \\ \cdots\cdots\cdots\cdots\cdots \\ w_{n1} & w_{n2} & \cdots & w_{nn} \end{bmatrix}$$

is multiplied by the matrix A above to obtain the state one utility assignments for each alternative for every individual, that is, WA is a matrix of state one utilities. State two utilities are obtained by multiplying W by WA, that is, by W^2A, and, in general, state n is equal to W^nA. Under the conditions described, as n goes to infinity, the process converges toward a set of consensual utilities. This occurs because as n goes to infinity, the weight matrix converges toward the vector of consensual weights, C, used to find the consensual utilities above.

As is obvious, we have, in this chapter, simply reversed the order of exposition from that of Chapter Two in order to apply the elementary model. Our reason for doing so is that the aggregation of utility assignments is more controversial than the aggregation of probability assignments as a method of amalgamating information. It may be difficult, in some contexts, to find a reasonable method for measuring utilities suitable for averaging as we shall explain below. In cases in which it is not feasible to compute suitable utilities for averaging but is feasible to compute consensual weights, we advocate using the social information summarized in the weights by whichever of our earlier described methods seems most appropriate to find consensus. In the case in which suitable utility assignments for averaging are available, we advocate our method for aggregating utility assignments on the grounds that by doing so we amalgamate the relevant information summarized in the utilities and weights individuals assign.

7. FROM CONSENSUAL UTILITIES TO ORDERINGS

Starting from the input of utilities and weights, we obtain a consensual ordering in a natural way. We require that an alternative A_j be preferred to A_k in the consensual ordering if and only if the consensual utility $u(A_j)$ is greater than the consensual utility $u(A_k)$. It is customary to distinguish between such preference, which is strict preference, and weak preference, which is equivalent to the disjunction of strict preference or indifference. We may then require that an alternative A_j be weakly preferred to A_k in the social ordering if and only if $u(A_j)$ is at least as great as $u(A_k)$. By imposing these conditions, we obtain a mapping from weights and utilities as input to a consensual ordering, which is referred to as a social welfare functional by Sen [1977] in the social choice literature. Harsanyi defended weighted averaging in [1976], [1977].

We need now confront the problem of deciding what sort of procedures could be used to ascertain the appropriate sort of individual utility functions as input. Unfortunately, the subjective or personalist method for ascertaining individual utility functions is not suitable in this context. That method, discovered by Ramsey [1931], yield utility functions that are unique up to positive linear or affine transformation. The method we have advocated requires greater rigidity. To understand what sort of individual utility assignments are required, it will be useful to consider three properties of the method we propose, considered as axiomatic constraints. We shall discuss these axioms with greater technical precision in chapter 6 with respect to the work of Gevers [1979].

8. THREE AXIOMS

The first of the axioms is the Strong Pareto Condition which says that if all individuals assign at least as high a utility to alternative j as to alternative k, that is, if a_{ij} is at least as great as a_{ik} for every individual i, then alternative j is weakly preferred to alternative to k in the consensual ordering. Moreover, if there is any individual that assigns j a higher utility than k, and all the others assign alternative j at least as high a utility as k, then j is strictly preferred to k in the consensual ordering. The second axiom is the Independence of Irrelevant alternatives that tells us that if two alternatives j and k have a different consensual ordering with respect to each other on a first set of individual utility assignments than on a second set, then there must be some difference in the individual utilities assigned to j and k on the two individual utility assignments. Conversely stated, if the two alternatives have exactly the same individual utilities assigned to them on two sets of individual utility assignments to alternatives, then they have the same consensual ordering with respect to each other on both assignments. This amounts to telling us that changes in the utilities assigned to other alternatives will not effect the consensual ordering of two alternatives with respect to each other when the utilities of those alternatives assigned by all individuals remain unchanged. The third axiom is Translation Invariance which tells us that adding a constant number to the utilities assigned to all alternatives by an individual will not alter the consensual ordering of alternatives. This condition can easily be seen to be a natural one. If person i assigns utilities to a set of k alternatives, so he has a_{i1}, a_{i2} and so forth, and he then adds some constant b to these alternatives so that he has instead $a_{i1}+b$, $a_{i2}+b$, this will have no influence on a weighted average of the utilities individuals assign. Person i will have given the same amount extra, so to speak, to each of the alternatives. Consequently, no alternative will be favored in the weighted averaging of the alternatives.

9. INDIVIDUAL UTILITIES

From the foregoing considerations, and especially from the axiom of Translation Invariance, we can clarify the necessary constraints on the sort of assignment of individual utilities that make the method applicable. We shall again discuss these matters in greater detail in chapter 6, but we note here that our aggregation method requires that the choice of a unit for measuring utilities be the same for all members of the group, though the choice of a zero point need not be the same. One immediate consequence, referred to above, is that the standard subjective or personalist method for determining individual utility assignments is not applicable. According to this method, an individual ascertains his utility assignment by assigning the value 1 to the most preferred alternative, 0 to the least preferred alternative, and the values of other alternatives are scaled in between with gambles. The value of such an intermediate alternative is equal to the probability at which the person is indifferent between accepting the alternative in question and a gamble at the probability in question when he will receive the most preferred alternative if he wins and the least preferred alternative if he loses. Such utility assignments have the advantage that they may be extracted from a sufficiently complete articulation of preferences among gambles, but they have the feature that they are unique only up to a positive linear or affine transformation. The informational content of such utility measures remains the same when the utilities are multiplied by any positive constant and any constant is also added. When we multiply the assignments of different individuals by different constants, they would not have the same unit of measurement. Since such assignments are only unique up to a positive linear or affine transformation, it would be arbitrary to disallow such multiplication. Thus the subjectivist or personalist method for measuring individual utilities yields results that are insufficiently unique or rigid, mathematically speaking, for the application of a method of weighted averaging. This result confirms Arrow's [1963] objection to employing such utility functions as the input for social choice.

10. INTERPERSONAL COMPARISON

This consideration brings us to the problem of finding some unit by which individuals can measure their utilities, and, hence, to the so called problem of the interpersonal comparison of utilities. As in the case of assigning weights, we do not offer or mandate any single method by which individuals should score alternatives to arrive at individual utility assignments. We do, however, wish to offer some relevant considerations. First of all, we contend that individuals do, in fact, often have information about the comparative intensity of preferences of others, just as they have information about the comparative intensity of other psychological states, pains for example. The problem is not that such information is lacking but that we must regiment it in some way. Secondly, we contend that it is not necessary that the unit of measurement be operationally defined in terms of some external standard or some physiological correlate in order to obtain a common unit. Thirdly, we note that the application of weights to utilities affords us the opportunity to correct what we may regard as errors or excesses at the level of assigning utilities.

There are, of course, diverse scoring systems for evaluating alternatives. We regard it as an empirical question which methods yield the highest degree of interpersonal stability. For example, the question of whether a scale with three levels or a hundred gives us greater interpersonal stability, that is, more closely comparable units for individuals, is one that goes beyond the limits of normative and formal inquiry. To this subject we have, therefore, no contribution to offer. We do note, however, that common conceptual and linguistic understanding may provide the basis for an initial, though empirically defeasible, assumption of comparable units. Thus, for example, if people are asked to rate alternatives as very good, good, neither good nor bad, bad, very bad, we may assume, initially, that they mean the same by these locutions, and, therefore, that scores assigned for each of these evaluations have the same meaning for the various individuals. Of course, this initial assumption may be refuted by further data, but then such data can be used to correct for the differences in meaning thus discovered. Moreover, if the individuals agree that difference between the various levels are the same, that is, for example, that a very good alternative is as much better than a merely good alternatives as a good alternative is better than a neither good nor bad alternative, and so on for other comparisons between other levels, then we may initially assume that the differences are comparable, and, consequently, that such a difference constitutes a comparable unit. This method was suggested by S. Lieberson (in discussion).

We do not, of course, claim that this system of grading would yield such comparable differences. It is the task of an empirical scientist to find a system of scoring where the numerical scores are correlated with descriptions in such way that people would agree that the differences between different levels are comparable. Moreover, we admit that further information might lead to the conclusion that people did not mean the same thing by the empirical descriptors associated with the numerical scores and that the initial assumption must be corrected. The initial assumption of comparability is empirically defeasible. That is, however, no argument against such an assumption. Empirical claims are, in general, defeasible, and this fact forces us to proceed in inquiry without the security of certainty. The defeasibility of an assumption may be a reason for further investigation, but it is not a reason for rejecting the assumption. Thus, we see no reason in principle for rejecting the assumption that comparable units for measuring intensity of preference may be found. The common understanding of descriptors among different individuals provides that basis for finding units of psychological measurement, and investigation in the social sciences rests on this basis. Such units may also serve as the basis for finding rational consensus.

The initial assumption of common understanding and comparable units derived therefrom is grounded on the methodological precept of simplicity. It is methodologically simpler to suppose that there is as much uniformity as is consistent with the empirical data than to suppose otherwise. There may be some controversy about how to interpret the requisite concept of simplicity, but the extrapolation of hypotheses and theories from empirical data depends on the practise of assuming as much uniformity as is consistent with such data. Of course, hypotheses and theories are defeasible and may be refuted by further investigation. Our contention is that when a common understanding of the meaning of expressions is unrefuted by the data, then this assumption is methodologically warranted. We leave the discovery of the interpersonally comparable unit of preference and other psychological states to the experts. We content ourselves with arguing that there is no good reason for pessimism about the outcome. We refer the reader to Harsanyi [1976], [1977] and Lehrer [1978] for further argumentation.

11. CORRECTIVE WEIGHTING

We note, finally, that one aspect of the problem of interpersonal comparison stems, not from a difficulty about finding a common unit of measurement, but rather from anxiety about how such a unit might be applied. Thus, even if we assume that individuals mean the same thing when they assign an alternative a given score, a score of 5 for example, and even if the difference between a score of 4 and 5 means the same for all, it remains possible that one person is inclined to have very extreme preferences, preferences that are felt to be excessively extreme by other members of the group. Thus, for example, on a scale of 1 to 5, people who always assign alternatives either a score of 1 or 5 appear unreasonable. It is absolutely critical to separate this problem from the problem of finding a unit of measurement. The fact that individuals have the same unit of measurement in no way insures that their preferences will not be unreasonably extreme or peculiar in some other way. It also does not insure that they will be honest and not exaggerate in reporting their preferences. Comparable units cannot be expected to eliminate intractable human failings.

Our method of weighting the utility of assignments of others provides us with the solution to the problem of exaggerated or extreme utility assignments. The solution is to discount others in the weight that is assigned to them when we believe that preferences are unreasonably extreme or when we believe that their reporting of their preferences is exaggerated. This is the stage at which our social information about others may be brought to bear. It might be useful to have some external standard or physiological correlate by which one could evaluate the intensity of preferences, pains and other psychological states. As philosophers have pointed out, however, the discovery of an appropriate standard or correlate depends on our having antecedent information about the intensity of such states in ourselves and others. If we did not have any means for ascertaining the intensity of preferences antecedently, we would lack the information needed to correlate intensity of preference with an external standard or physiological state. Such a standard or correlate, once discovered, might well enable us to refine and make more precise our information about the intensity of others psychological states. The epistemological order of discovery in these matters, however, requires that we first have some initial unregimented information about such matters before we can discover the appropriate standard or correlate. Assuming, therefore, that we have such knowledge, we are in position to evaluate the utility assignments of others, to assign weights based on such information, and to discount assignments that seem to us defective.

12. SUMMARY

Thus, we consider it essential to draw a distinction between two aspects of the problem of the interpersonal comparison of utilities. The first problem is to find some comparable unit of utility. We allege, as method, that it is reasonable to initially assume a common understanding of expressions describing intensity. We admit that such an assumption is defeasible but note that this does not distinguish this assumption from scientific claims generally. Given this initial assumption, or one corrected for differences discovered in understanding among individuals, the discovery of a comparable unit of utility appropriate to a specific decision problem becomes a matter of empirical investigation. Even if people have an interpersonally comparable unit of measurement to apply, the utilities they report may be defective in at least two important ways. They may report their utilities incorrectly, just as one may report measurements with a ruler incorrectly, either because they seek to mislead others or because they have not been sufficiently attentive to the measurement process. Moreover, even if one has reported accurately, the intensities themselves may seem to us unreasonable. For example, one person may always assign either very low or very high utilities, another may always assign high utilities, another always very low, and yet another may assign middle utilities only. When we are interested in reaching a decision that will yield the best alternative, and when we are considering the utility assignments of individuals as a representation of rational evaluations of how good the alternatives are, we may choose to discount evaluations that exhibit some constant pattern over time regardless of the issue to be decided. We may judge that such utility assignments are not a reliable guide to what is best and discount them accordingly.

Thus, the problem of the interpersonal comparison of utilities is a combination of three problems rather than a single one. We must find a comparable unit, then correct for inaccurate reporting, and finally discount some unreasonable intensities. An external standard or physiological correlate of the unit would be useful for dealing with the first two problems, but for the third, the use of weights remains essential. The most objective formulation or measurement of preferences we could imagine would not in any way guarantee that each individual would be an equally reliable guide to what is best. We would still be left with the usual distribution of fools and geniuses, knaves and saints, as before. The need to evaluate them, to assign different weights to their utilities, would remain.

There are cases, however, in which all parties will be assigned equal consensual weight. We are then left with a problem of social choice in which the sole determinant will be individual preferences or individual utility scales. The question then arises as to whether we should use the individual utility scales or whether we are forced to use only individual preferences? We think that the discovery that consensual weights are equal should not lead to the conclusion that utility scales should be disregarded. Instead, egalitarian consensual weighting indicates the appropriate use of the utility scales for social choice. If a utility scale seems extreme, or if a utility scale seems inaccurate, these defects will be discounted in the consensual weights assigned to the people in question. The fact that consensual weights are equal justifies us in concluding that, according to the consensus of the group, there are no such discrepancies. Hence, consensual egality in weighting indicates the use of the utility scales is appropriate for social choice. In this instance, a simple average yields the social ordering.

We do, however, acknowledge situations where social choice must be based on the amalgamation of individual preferences alone as Arrow proposed in [1951]. For example, if members of the group are duplicious in such a way that others cannot discount their dupliciousness in any acceptable way, then communication of respect may collapse. The aggregate group may decompose into small units, as small as single membered groups composed of one maximally self-respecting member. Here ethical anarchy obtains, and there are no consensual weights. We have, in this instance, no evaluation of the utility scales, and, therefore, no method for discounting exaggeration or unreasonably extreme assignments.

Arrow's proposal of [1951], which we discuss in Chapter 6, reflects a more pragmatic and realistic and less normative and idealized construal of the problem of social choice as the amalgamation of individual preferences. In the usual case of social choice, no one has presented a utility scale, and people might be unable or unwilling to do so. They surely will not have assigned numerical weights to others. Arrow's construal of the problem is less idealized. It does contain some degree of idealization, however. It requires that people articulate preferences among things they might not have compared and might find difficult to compare. More critically, it imposes rational normative constraints on the permitted structure of the preferences. For example, it is required that strict preference and indifference be transitive. This is, as others have noted, a nontrivial constraint. Indifference may fail to be transitive because of threshold features of observation. A person who cannot discern any difference between A and B, or between B and C, and, hence, is indifferent between each of those pairs, may be able to discern a difference between A and C, the difference here rising above the minimal threshold. In such cases, indifference is not actually transitive. The requirement that indifference be transitive is a normative imposition.

The foregoing remarks are not to be understood as objections to such constraints on preference and indifference. On the contrary, it is our conviction that transitivity is a proper normative constraint. It is, however, *normative*, a condition of rationality. The assumption that people have preferences satisfying such constraints is an idealization. Once one begins imposing normative constraints, one requires people to diverge from actual practise to conform to rationality. When it is a rational methodology that one is proposing, it seems reasonable to us to consider all the rational constraints that could be met. Choice that fails to meet the constraints imposed falls short of perfect rationality. Such rationality provides us with an ideal to which actual practise can aspire, if time and resources allow, or approximate when they do not. Social choice among alternatives based on individual preferences among alternatives alone falls short of the ideal of rationality requiring that rational decision be based on all the relevant information available. There may, however, be a great number of situations that place sufficiently severe restraints on time and other resources so that no more information than preferences of individuals may be employed. Many voting situations are of this sort, for example. On the other hand, weights and utilities supply additional information when they can be provided. The use of such information more nearly approaches ideally rational decision making.

CHAPTER FOUR

THE EXTENDED MODEL

In this chapter we present a more sophisticated version of the model elaborated in the last two chapters. We call it the *extended* model, and it is an improvement over the elementary model in two important respects. First of all, the constancy condition is dropped, that is, we allow that members of the group might assign different weights at higher levels of evaluation. Secondly, we propose a method for regimenting discussion at different levels of evaluation to insure proper separation of issues. We then discuss the conditions under which the process of aggregation converges toward a limit, thus yielding a set of consensual weights. We then note that such a set of weights can be computed and justified without the assumption of infinitely iterated aggregation and, therefore, that it is unnecessary to assume an infinite hierarchy of weights. Finally, we turn to the question of whether an individual is rationally committed to the consensus our methods yield. We argue that, given that he assigns weights so consensus is reached, he is committed to the outcome. We note, however, that an individual may escape such a commitment by assigning others a weight of zero at some level, and thus refuse to generate consensus. We conclude with a discussion of the merits of iconoclasm.

1. CONSTANCY ABANDONED

The model for the selection of consensual probability and utility assignments articulated in the previous two chapters used a constancy condition to obtain convergence, namely, the condition that the weights assigned to each level be the same. Note that this was a synchronic assumption, for it is clear that the weights, as well as other measures, might be altered across time or with the acquisition of new information. Even the assumption of synchronic constancy is, however, overly restrictive as a requirement of rationality. We shall now drop this constraint, by so doing complicate our model, and explain how convergence may be obtained without it.

We used the constancy assumption to justify the process of aggregation on grounds of consistency and the use of information. Refusal to aggregate at any stage is equivalent to assigning zero weight to other members of the group and aggregating. Assuming that a person does not assign zero weight to all members of the group, and assuming the constancy condition, consistency and an interest in using relevant information requires that the person aggregate at each level. When the respect condition is met, aggregation drives the group toward a consensual assignment.

Why is it necessary to drop the constancy requirement? The reason is that the weights assigned to a person at different levels represent different judgments about the person. Suppose that an individual has arrived at an aggregated state one probability assignment by one round of averaging. His assignment is equal to the following: $w_{j1}p_1 + w_{j2}p_2 + \ldots + w_{jn}p_n = p_j^1$. Suppose i considers what weight to assign to this stage one probability assignment of person j. When i assigns a weight to this probability assignment, i has already evaluated the first level probability assignments, so i should assign a weight to the weights that person j has assigned to each member of the group. To compute a stage two probability assignment, i computes a sum of products of the form $w_{ij}^1 w_{jk}^0 p_k$. Having evaluated p_k at the first level, i is now evaluating w_{jk}^0, that is, person i is assigning a weight to the weight that person j assigned to others at the first level.

Less mathematically formulated, the second level weight is the weight that person i assigns to person j as a judge of others. So, if the problem is the astronomical one mentioned earlier, the weight that person i assigns to the initial probability assignment of j articulates his opinion of how good a solar astronomer j is. Once a person arrives at a stage one probability assignment, his assignment expresses his opinion about the merits of members of the group as solar astronomers. For his assignment at stage one is a weighted average of initial probability assignments of others. The weights express his opinion about the merits of members of the group as solar astronomers. So when person i decides what weight to assign the stage one probability assignment of j, person i is assigning a weight to the weight that j assigns to members of the group as solar astronomers. In other words, at stage one, i is judging j as a judge of solar astronomers rather than as a judge of solar astronomy. It is clear that this is a different judgment that might employ different information. For, person i might think that person j is an excellent solar astronomer but a poor judge of the expertise of others, or, on the contrary, person i might think that j is not a very good solar astronomer but an excellent judge of solar astronomers. If either of these differences exist, then the initial stage weight that i assigns to j, w_{ij}^0, might differ from his stage one weight, w_{ij}^1. Of course, the same applies to the stage two weight, w_{ij}^2, which expresses i's evaluation of j as a judge of judges of astronomers rather than as a judge of astronomers.

Another aid to understanding the weights at different stages or levels is to think of the initial weight as the weight i gives to j as a member of a committee to arrive at an answer to a question in solar astronomy. The stage one weight i gives to j is the weight that i gives to j as a member of a panel who are going to select a committee to answer the question in solar astronomy. Of course, the stage two weights are the weights that person i gives to j as a member of a higher level panel to select the previous panel, and so on for higher level weights. At each stage the weight assigned reflects a different judgment, and it is at least possible in principle that different information could be used at each stage of weighting.

2. AGGREGATION UNDER INCONSTANCY

The constancy condition is not necessary as a premise in an argument for aggregation. To sustain aggregation, we need only the assumption that a person assigns some positive weight to others at each stage. Dropping the constancy requirement deletes one reason for aggregating, but that reason is readily replaced. If we may suppose that a person gives some weight to others as solar astronomers, we may also suppose that he will give some weight to others as judges of solar astronomers. To refuse to assign any positive weight to others at stage one is equivalent to assigning zero weight to everyone else as a judge of solar astronomers and aggregating. If, in fact, the person does not assign zero weight to others as judges of solar astronomers, then refusal to aggregate, since it is equivalent to assigning a weight of zero to others and aggregating, is inconsistent. In the elementary model we do not require that a person assign positive weight to others as a condition of rationality. It may, as we have noted, be reasonable in some situations to assign a weight of zero to everyone else. We think such situations should be rare but not impossible. What we do require as a condition of rationality is that one consistently follow out the consequences of assigning positive weight to others by aggregating.

Our conjecture is that a person who assigns some weight to others as solar astronomers will also assign some positive weight to others as judges of solar astronomers and so forth. Our reasoning is that a person who is willing to give some weight to the views of others about solar astronomy will be willing to give some weight to their views about solar astronomers as well. There is, however, no proof that this must be so. It is logically consistent for a person to hold the position that the opinions of others about solar astronomy have some worth but the opinions of others about solar astronomers are entirely worthless. It is, though consistent, odd. A person who is conceded to have some merit as a solar astronomer would, ordinarily, have some merit as a judge of solar astronomers, because he could use his knowledge of solar astronomy to judge the virtues of others as solar astronomers. A person might prove unable to apply his knowledge of the subject to evaluate the expertise of others, but we would expect this to be rare. Consequently, we would expect that people who assign positive weight to others initially should do so subsequently.

Moreover, the fact that weights at different stages or levels express information about different questions enhances the argument for aggregating beyond the first level. In the elementary model, a critic might object that having assigned a weight at the initial stage and aggregated, he can see no merit in reapplying the same weight. For, he might object, having already given a weight to the opinion of another, he does not see any reason to repeat. He might protest that information expressed in his initial weight has been exhausted or completely utilized at the first stage of aggregation. Having given positive weight to others, he might refuse to give them that weight again, and, therefore, assign them a weight of zero subsequently.

3. STRATIFIED WEIGHTING

Whatever merit there is to the objection of such a critic is overcome by use of the extended model. On that model, the weight given at each stage is a weight given to a person for a different opinion, different information. This can be made clear by imagining a more stratified and regimented form of discussion proposed by Wagner [1978] resembling the Delphi method. Suppose that the group of people involved, our solar astronomers for example, first communicated with each other by writing anonymous position papers on the astronomical question at issue, the shape of the sun for example. After the merits of such discussion are conceded to be exhausted, after dialectical equilibrium is reached at this level, the group assigns probabilities and the authors of the position papers are revealed. If consensus is not reached, they exchange another round of anonymous position papers, this time concerned with the question of how good a solar astronomer each member of the group was. When this exchange of information reaches a stage of dialectical equilibrium, each person uses the information about others to assign a weight to members of the group as solar astronomers and authors of the position papers are revealed. If aggregation at this stage produces consensus, the process terminates. If not, the group exchanges another round of anonymous position papers, this time addressed to the question of how good a judge of solar astronomers each person was. When this exchange of papers reaches dialectical equilibrium, members of the group assign weights to members as judges of solar astronomers and authors of the position papers are revealed. If consensus is reached by aggregation with these weights, then the process is terminated, if not, another round of anonymous position papers is exchanged addressed to the question of how good a judge of judges of solar astronomers each person is, and so on.

This process, though it could not be carried on infinitely, clarifies two features. First, weights beyond the first level articulate genuinely new information. Therefore, having assigned a weight at the first level does not warrant a person claiming that he has done all he can to express the relevant information he possesses at the initial stage and refusing to assign any positive weight to others after the first stage. Such a person is refusing to articulate information that he possesses, or, at least, he may be doing so. Second, one must imagine that, at some stage, there will be no new information. In the exchange of position papers, nothing new will be forthcoming. At this point, it would be unreasonable, in our opinion, for a person to go on shifting weights. If there is no new information available, for example, about people as judges of judges of astronomers over and above what was available about them as judges of astronomers, then we conclude that the same weight should be assigned to a person as a judge of judges of astronomers as was assigned to him as a judge of astronomers, and so on for higher levels. One other possible variation is for a person who is unable to discriminate between one person and another at some level to assign all members of the group equal weights. Our assumption is that the more reasonable method would be for a person to assign the same weights at higher levels that he assigned at the last level at which he had any information he considered to be relevant. However, there is no decisive argument, we concede, for disallowing a person to become egalitarian when he has no additional information.

4. CONVERGENCE UNDER INCONSTANCY

In Chapter Eight, we shall examine in mathematical detail the various conditions under which convergence occurs, that is, under which the weights that individuals assign converge toward a set of consensual weights. When we undertake that examination, we shall note that it is not at all necessary to assume that the weights that are assigned remain constant for individuals past a certain point. Assuming communication of respect in the weights assigned at each level, it will suffice for convergence that the set of smallest entries in the matrices, u_1, u_2, and so forth are such that the sequence of numbers u_1, u_1+u_2, $u_1+u_2+u_3$ and so forth increase without bound. Indeed, it will even suffice if the result of taking the products of consecutive blocks of matrices that communicate respect yields a set of matrices whose smallest entries satisfy this condition. It is, however, plausible to suppose that at some level members of the group will run out of further information and either assign the same weights at higher levels that they assign at the last level at which they had relevant information, or shift to the egalitarian scheme. We note here that if all members become constant after a certain point, and if there is communication of respect at the level at which constancy is instituted, then there is convergence. A consensual set of weights results.

There are other important mathematical features of the model. First of all, once consensus occurs, it cannot be dislodged by proceeding to a higher level of weights. Mathematically, this means that if matrix W_j is multiplied by W_i, and W_i is a consensus matrix in which each person has the same row of weights for members of the group, then the product W_jW_i, equals W_i. The multiplication by the higher level matrix produces no alteration. This is critical. It proves that though our model can produce consensus when none has been found by other methods, but it cannot destroy a consensus once one has been found. The same observation pertains to the original probability or utility assignment. If there is agreement to begin with, aggregating will yield back that agreement unaltered. Thus, those who are inclined to think that the original probability and utility assignments are closer to hard data and empirical evidence, with first level weights being evidentially much more tenuous and higher level weights being even more so, should be reassurred that any agreement that can be obtained from the sort of evidence he favors cannot be dislodged by aggregation.

Indeed, the foregoing consideration provides a reply to a critic who objects to aggregation. If there is disagreement on the basis of experimental data, then such data does not provide us with any answer to the question of what probability or utility assignment is indicated by the data considered. Consider the example of the probability of a hypothesis. When there is disagreement, all the evidence allows us to conclude is that the probability assignment lies in the interval between the highest and lowest assigned. Aggregation uses further information, social information about expertise and reliability of members of the group, but the consensual assignment, if there is one, must fall in the original interval. Our method guarantees this. If there is agreement, then the upper and lower bound of the interval are the same, and that must be the consensual assignment no matter what weights are assigned. This argument can be duplicated with respect to weights. The weights assigned to a given member at the first stage will, if there is disagreement, contain a lowest and a highest weight for the individual. The consensual weight assigned to the person must be in that interval. Thus, turning to higher level weights must preserve what agreement there is at the lower level. Aggregation can decrease disagreement; it cannot increase it.

In short, our argument for aggregation is this. Suppose you are interested in obtaining a single point summary of the information members of the group possess. If the experimental data yields such a summary, our method preserves it. If the experimental data does not yield such a summary, then, if respect is communicated, our method uses social information to obtain the summary. One may, of course, not be interested in determining what the most reasonable probability or utility is on the basis of the information available to the group. Then no method for finding such a summary is needed. If one raises the question of what all the information adds up to, our method provides the answer when respect is communicated. It does not go beyond our information. It uses the totality of informaton and preserves the answers we have obtained.

Moreover, just as consensus once obtained is preserved, so consensus finally obtained at a higher level insures convergence in the process of aggregation. If W_j is a matrix in which each member assigns the same row of weights to members of the group, then the result of multiplying W_j times W_i, the product W_jW_i, is also a consensus matrix, though not the same as W_j necessarily. What this means is that if at any stage in the aggregation procedure each person assigns the same row of weights, then convergence immediately results. What the convergent values will be is determined by all the preceding stages of aggregation, but agreement at any level suffices to yield a consensual assignment. Thus, if every member of the group becomes egalitarian after some level stage of aggregation, that would insure convergence at that stage without proceeding to higher levels.

The foregoing result yields an important consequence for applications of our method across time when new information is obtained at the first level. Suppose aggregation beyond a certain level converges as aggregation goes to infinity toward some consensual set of weights for the group. If there is some new information that leads to a change in the initial probabilities or utilities but does not lead to any alteration of the weights members of the group assign to each other, then we are assured that aggregation yields consensus. If there is a change in the first level weights as well, convergence is still guaranteed if the weights originally assigned beyond the first level converge as aggregation goes to infinity. Thus, if there is convergence of this sort from stage i, then alteration below that level will still yield convergence. Thus, appraisal at higher levels, providing it is convergent and constant across time, will insure consensus.

5. CONSENSUS WITHOUT ITERATION

It is important here to consider a method for computing consensual weights corresponding to those obtained in the elementary model without infinitely aggregating. It is a theorem, to be discussed in detail in chapter 7, that the set of consensual weights C reached by infinitely iterated multiplication of a matrix of weights W (communication of respect being assumed) is unique in that multiplying C by W, CW, yields C as a result. In other words, when we use the set of consensual weights, w_1, w_2, and so forth to w_n to average the weights w_{1j}, w_{2j}, and so forth to w_{nj}, originally assigned to j, we find that $w_1 w_{1j} + w_2 w_{2j} + \ldots + w_n w_{nj} = w_j$. This set of consensual weights is called a *fixed point vector* for the matrix, and communication of respect guarantees that there is exactly one such vector. As result, it is possible to find the consensual weights for such a matrix by solving a small number of linear equations instead of directly computing the limit toward which the iterated multiplication of the matrix converges. Of course, the fixed point vector is that limit.

Other than the nicety of computation, the fixed point vector allows us to give an argument for using the consensual weights for finding consensus that is independent of continued aggregation. This is important for the following reason. Once a stage is reached where people do not have further new information to add at higher levels, the argument for aggregation is somewhat weaker. It may be necessary to continue aggregation to obtain a summary of the total information in the form of single probability or utility assignment. If, however, higher level weights beyond a certain level add no new information, then what justification do we have for using the set of limit weights derived from higher level weights to represent a consensus?

The answer to the foregoing question can be found if we consider what mathematical features an acceptable set of consensual weights must have. Returning once again to the solar astronomer example, imagine that we have aggregated using initial state weights, W^0, and have thus found a state one probability assignment, P^1. We now find, when we proceed to higher levels, that though members of the group were able to bring new information to bear to distinguish between members as solar astronomers and judges of solar astronomers, they are unable to bring any new information to bear to distinguish between members as judges of astronomers and judges of judges of astronomers. Thus, though the initial state weights, W^0, used to compute the first level probability assignment, P^1, differ from the state one weights, W^1, the latter weights are identical with state two weights, W^2, because no new information can be brought to bear to distinguish between them. If we continue to aggregate with the W^1 matrix, we converge toward a set of limit weights which we can multiply times P^1 to obtain a consensual result, but we seem to lack a cogent argument for the iterated aggregation.

Suppose, however, we pose the question of what set of weights would be the best set of weights we could find to average P^1 in order to represent consensus. Imagine that a set L consisting of 1_1, 1_2, and so forth to 1_n is proposed. Note that since W^1 contains relevant social information, the result of using L to average P^1 would have to be the same as the result of first using W^1 to average P^1, thus arriving at state two probability P^2, and then using L to average P^2. Thus, LP^1 must equal LP^2, or else relevant information contained in W^1 would make a relevant difference in the outcome proving that L was an inappropriate set of weights to average the state one probabilities, P^1, in order to represent a consensus based on the relevant social information. In other words, if L is an appropriate set of consensual weights to represent the social information, then $LP^1 = L(W^1P^1)$ in that $P^2 = W^1P^1$. From this it follows, as we show in chapter 7, that $LW^1 = L$, and, consequently, that L must be the fixed point vector for W^1, assuming respect is communicated in the matrix. Thus, L is an appropriate set of weights for averaging P^1 if and only if L is the set of weights C that is the limit toward which infinitely iterated multiplication of the matrix W^1 converges. So, we have a justification for using C to find the consensus based on the social information without using weights beyond level W^1, the last level at which new information is brought to bear. This result can be looked upon as either a justification for using the values obtained from infinitely iterated aggregation or as an alternative method of limited aggregation yielding the same result.

There remains one objection suggesting the model might require further complication. We have noted that, at stage two, person i is evaluating other members of the group as evaluators. So, at that stage, when person i assigns a weight to person j, say to the weight that j assigns to k, W_{jk}, person i is assigning a weight to j as an evaluator of k. Now it may have occurred to someone to suggest that the weight that person i assigns to j as an evaluator of k might differ from the weight that person i assigns to j as an evaluator of some other person, because person i thinks that j is a better or worse evaluator of k than of other persons. It must be conceded, of course, that in everyday affairs a person may be a better evaluator of one person than another. This can arise in two ways. First, one may have better information about one than another, or secondly, he may be more honest in evaluating one person than another. The first consideration is eliminated on our model by the restriction of dialectical equilibrium, whether reached in open discussion or through discussion papers. Consequently, each member of the group must be assumed to have the same information about every individual that every other member of the group has. With respect to the second condition, we require for the use of the model that members be impartial and disinterested in their evaluation of others. If, in fact, someone is judged to be prejudiced, then his evaluations of others must be discounted and communication of respect to that person fails. The situation is like one in which someone has been dishonest in reporting experimental results. Though it is unfortunate to be forced to disregard all the results such a person reports, once the person is known to be dishonest, all of his experimental reports must be called into question until they can be independently validated. Thus, when person i assigns some weight to j as an evaluator of k, person i need only be concerned with j as an evaluator of others and assign to j whatever weight it is appropriate to assign to j as such an evaluator in comparison to other members of the group.

6. COMMITMENT TO CONSENSUS

We now turn to the question of whether the members of a group are rationally committed to accepting the consensual result. To answer this question, it is important to note that there is more than one way to assign a weight to another. One may assign the weight in either an egoistic or a disinterested manner. A person assigns a weight to another egoistically when the weight assigned simply represents how nearly the other person agrees with him or is otherwise chosen simply to make his own opinion prevail in the aggregation. If an egoistic weighter knows someone to be expert and reliable in the subject under consideration but disagrees with that person in this instance, then the egoistic weighter will assign such a person a much lower weight than he would assign to someone with whom he agrees but knows to be inept and usually unreliable. The disinterested weighter will assign weights to others in terms of how expert and reliable they are in the subject at hand rather than in terms of how closely they agree with him. The disinterested weighter, if he thinks he is the more reliable and expert member of the group, may assign himself the highest weight, but others will be evaluated in terms of their reliability and expertise rather than proximity to his opinion.

We require that the weights be assigned in a disinterested manner. When that requirement is met, the consensual opinion is, we contend, a rational summary of the total information contained in the group. It is superior to a simple average for the reason that it uses more information. The need for using such information becomes apparent when one again reflects that some person in the group might assign a very high probability to a hypothesis, a very high utility to an alternative, or a very high weight to some member of the group, when there is a consensus that such a person is very unreliable about the subject and about the reliability of others. If we take a simple average of probabilities, utilities or the weights assigned to a person to find the consensual probability, utility or weight, then the high probability, utility or weight assigned by the inept party will have an excessively strong influence on the outcome. On the interated aggregation procedure described above, however, the values assigned by such a person will be discounted in the aggregation process. Since he will receive a small consensual weight, the probability, utility or weight he assigns will be given proportionately little weight.

7. DEFECTIVE INPUT

Thus, with the qualification sindicated, the consensual weight will be an appropriate and rational summary of the information contained in the group. Is each individual committed to the summary? That is, would it be irrational for any person contained in the group to refuse to alter his probability or utility assignment to match the consensual assignment when respect is communicated throughout the group? There are some conditions under which it would not be irrational. The first, and most obvious, is when the person, through lack of mathematical expertise, does not know the consensual outcome. Ignorance is a perfect excuse. Suppose, however, that the consensual outcome is made known to a member of the group and that it is reached through the communication of respect. Would it then be irrational for him to refuse to modify his probability or utility assignment to match the consensual one? Again we cannot claim that it would be irrational without qualification. Perhaps the procedure should not have been used. A person might be reasonably convinced that probabilities or utilities originally assigned were based on very little information or reflection. Similarly, he might believe that the weights members assigned to each other were based on little evidence. Or he might believe that the assignments of weights were egoistic rather than disinterested. He might think that he should have refused to participate in the process or that he should have assigned zero weight to others at some stage, though, in fact, he did not. In such a case, the person might regard the consensual probability as the aggregation of ignorance and prejudice. He might, therefore, demure at the suggestion that he match his probability or utility assignment with the consensual one. If his belief about the probabilities, utilities and weights is a reasonable one, then the input was defective, and it is obviously not irrational for him to refuse to conform to the resulting consensual output.

8. METHOD AS MEANS

However, the critical question is whether a member of the group is rationally committed to the consensual probability or utility assignment on the assumption that the individual probability and utility assignments are summaries of genuine information, that the weights are too, and, moreover, that the latter are assigned in a disinterested manner. Is the individual member of the group then rationally committed to the consensual outcome when it is made known to him?

It is clear that there is a philosophical and political tradition that answers the question affirmatively. The presupposition is that *if* you enter into certain rational processes, you are rationally committed to the outcome. One may disagree about the process. But once we agree that the method for obtaining some end, whether truth and freedom from error, or security and freedom from fear, is rational, we are rationally committed to the outcome. The general assumption is that one who is rationally committed to a certain means is rationally committed to the end that subsequently results. In the model in question, therefore, if a person is rationally committed to aggregating the information summarized in individual probabilities utilities and weights to obtain the most rational overall summary of such information contained in the group, then he is rationally committed to the outcome.

9. IRRATIONAL CONSENSUS

The foregoing reasoning, though it has the weight of authority behind it, is subject to a further objection. Refusal to conform to the most rational scheme, it may be argued, is sometimes appropriate. There is a tradition in the philosophy and historiography of science claiming the scientific iconoclast is the source of creative innovation. Similar remarks pertain to innovation in social policy. There is surely some evidence that individuals who have refused to conform to consensual authority in science and social policy have made highly significant contributions they might otherwise have failed to make. We require some reply to deal with this counterconsensual observation.

First, we note that the consensus contravened in these historical instances was not reached by the rational method we prescribe. Consensus reached by inferior methods is such that no one may be rationally committed to either the method or the outcome. This reply is important, for it is unlikely that consensual opinion in the past was based on an aggregation, even implicitly, of disinterested evaluations. Iconoclasts might have correctly thought that social authority was based on political power rather than on a rational aggregation of information. If social authority is not a rational consensus, is not the outcome of a rational method, then it is not rationally binding.

10. ICONOCLASM

One might yet object that even if the process we have described were employed to reach consensus, it would still be undesirable from a scientific and social point of view if all members of the scientific and social community were to conform to the consensus. The consensual probability will tend, being an average, to swamp the more extreme points of view. They will be pressed toward the center, and, therefore, iconoclasm will repressed. Instead, it might be contended, it is quite rational to maintain extreme points of view. By so doing one becomes scientifically adventurous, and such a strategy holds out richer prospects for finding some scientific innovation or social reform.

This sort of defense of scientific and social iconoclasm can be dealt with by our model. The defense of iconoclasm might be treated as an exhortation to discount the opinions of other to zero at some level in order to avoid being driven from one's iconoclastic outlook. We have not said that it is always unreasonable to assign others a weight of zero. Moreover, on the extended model it is possible to assign a weight of zero to others at any level of weighting and thereby destroy communication of respect and consensus in the group. To assign others a weight of zero on our model does not preclude taking them seriously or refusing to consider the evidence they possess. One might, having considered the opinions of others and, having evaluated their data, adjust the probability one assigns to a hypothesis or the utility one assigns to an alternative. One might then decide to give zero weight to them. There is danger of ambiguity here. One may give what one considers to be reasonable emphasis to the evidence and opinion of others in ones reflection about some scientific or social question, but, having come to a conclusion, refuse to assign a positive weight to any other conclusion. There is a good deal of conduct in science and society which appears to fit this strategy. For example, when a scientist listens to criticism of his theory, attempts to deal with the criticism in a reasonable way, but refuses to change his opinion, he then discounts the opinion of others and the weight they give to those who disagree with him. Similarly, a social reformer, though well informed about the values and preferences of the community as well as the reasons for them, may refuse to alter his preferences to align them with those that are prevalent. Such people may be looked upon as ones who assign a weight of zero to others and think that it is rational to do so. The question of when it is rational to assign others a weight of zero, and thus break oneself off from the process of consensual aggregation, is a fascinating one. Perhaps it is always reasonable to do so in science or social policy when one is convinced that others are misled in their opinions or preferences by some fundamental error.

11. CONSENSUAL CONFLICT

A difficult case of this sort would be one in which a person, who does give weight to others at the first level, knows the consensual outcome they would reach through the continued communication of respect at higher levels, and regards others as having information and being disinterested. Can it be rational for such a person to discount others to zero at a higher level to escape the need to conform? Suppose that a group of experts had reached the opinion, or assigned a very high probability, to the hypothesis that nonconformity, refusal to generate consensus, on the frontiers of a special discipline, for example, solar energy engineering, is more likely to produce effective technological advance than conformity to current methods. Moreover, suppose that you are a member of the group, and you are also a solar engineer. Other solar engineers reach consensus that a standard solar cell is very probably the most cost efficient cell that can be developed in the next ten years. You assign a much lower probability to this hypothesis because, though unable to persuade others, you have an idea for an entirely different kind of solar cell you think will have greater cost efficiency than the standard cell. You do, however, respect other members of the group, and, indeed, belong to a group in which respect is communicated throughout the group at the first level.

The question is what it is reasonable for you to do. You will be committed to the consensus if you assign positive weight to others at higher levels. You are very much at odds with the consensual probability assignment you know would result. Moreover, the group itself holds that nonconformity, refusal to generate consensus, is more likely to produce effective technological advances. In short, there is a consensus that, in this specific domain, it is reasonable not to conform to rationally reached consensus.

This problem cannot be resolved by a simple appeal to the distinction between what it is reasonable to believe and what it is reasonable to do. One might be tempted to suggest that the person should adopt the consensual probability but, when deciding what line of research to pursue, follow his own research path. We can, however, easily imagine that it would be unreasonable for him to attempt to develop the solar cell he conceives if he accepts the consensual probability. The expectation of success might be too low. Suppose that the utility of succeeding does not suffice to outweigh the very low consensual probability of achieving it. In this instance, we may imagine that it would be reasonable for him to attempt to develop his solar cell given the probability he assigns but not on the basis of the consensual probability. Here the choice between his personal probability and the consensual probability is critical. If p_i is his personal probability assignment and p_c is the consensual assignment, then his expectation, $e(A_i)$, given that he chooses course of action A_i based on p_i is $e(A_i) = p_i(S_1)u(O_{i1}) + p_i(S_2)u(O_{i2}) + \ldots + p_i(S_n)u(O_{in})$ where S_j is a possible state of nature occurring with A_i and O_{ij} is the outcome of S_j with A_i. Obviously, substituting p_c for p_i in the equation may yield different results and a different maximal act. The probability a person acts upon is the one he accepts if he is rational. It is unreasonable to accept a probability assignment and act as though the probabilities were otherwise.

This situation is a difficult one. Moreover, it is not unrealistic to imagine the person choosing his personal probability assignment. Since there is a consensus against generating consensus, the person is in conflict from the consensual point of view. There is an analogy here to higher order preferences. It is commonplace that one person may prefer that another person not have the preferences he does. I may prefer, if seated next to you, that you not prefer to smoke when, in fact, you do prefer to smoke. That is a conflict between my preference and your preference. But there may also be conflict between my preferences. I may prefer to smoke on a given occasion but prefer that I not have that preference. I may prefer that I prefer not to smoke, though, as a matter of unfortunate fact, I prefer to smoke. There is, in such a case, a conflict between my first order preference and my second order preference. Such preferential conflict is discussed by Frankfurt [1971] and Jeffrey [1974]. There is a similar conflict between preference in the consensual case. It would be natural to generate a consensus that the probability of a specific hypothesis is high. There is, however, a consensus that better results would be obtained by individuals not generating a consensual probability to be preferred to their personal probabilities in hypotheses of this kind. So there is a first level consensual preference for generating a high consensual probability for the hypothesis in question, but there is a second level consensual preference for not generating the consensually preferred probability for the hypothesis.

This sort of conflict is not amenable to any obvious sort of aggregation procedure because it is a conflict between levels. A person who is rationally committed to following a consensual directive is confronted with the same sort of conflict as the person who, in fact, prefers to smoke but would prefer not to have that preference. There is no simple formula for resolving such conflicts. A person who resolves the conflict by refusing to generate the consensual probability is not unreasonable. Neither is the person who generates consensus. When consensual authority is at conflict with itself, as we imagine in this instance, the individual lacks a rationally compelling directive.

Our conjecture is that such conflict is common, in science and ethics, where iconoclasts are heroes but everyone is taught to conform. The penalty for nonconformity may range from benign neglect to ostracism. The potential reward for conformity is acceptance and perhaps canonization. Consensual opinion is not to be blamed for placing the individual in this situation. The problem is that it is impossible to tell when nonconformity will be profitable. It is highly probable that some who refuse to conform will obtain the truth in science or a needed reform in social policy. It may be impossible to say who or when.

12. CONFLICTING CONSENSUAL GROUPS

The foregoing case is one in which there is conflict between different levels. It may also happen that a person aggregates with different groups that obtain different results. A person may find that aggregation within one group would lead to a different consensual probability or utility assignment than aggregation within another group. As we noted in Chapter Two, one individual is sufficient to join two groups into a composite group in which respect is communicated. For if each group to which he belongs is one that communicates respect, then the larger group communicates respect also, if only through that person. For example, if there is a chain of positive respect from each member of the first group to the person in question, and a chain of respect from that person to each member of the second group, then there is a chain of respect from each member of the first group though the person in question to each member of the second group. Though the consensual probability or utility of the combined group would be the most reasonable in that it aggregates the most information, it may not be possible for the person to discover the composite consensus. He may be ignorant of what weight members of one group would assign to members of the other group. Hence, he cannot determine the consensus for the combined group. In this instance, there may be two consensual groups with differing consensual probabilities for the same hypothesis. The person may lack any reasonable method for choosing the consensus of one group over another.

The preceding problem and the present one are both cases of conflict. They are closely related. The problem of individual iconoclasm may, in fact, be considered as simply a special case of conflict between the consensual probability or utility assignments of two groups. Individual iconoclasts may be thought of as comparing the probability or utility assignment of a unit group, containing only the iconoclast in question, with that of larger group for which a consensus is known. There is, however, one important difference. The individual who gives positive weight to members of a group that communicates respect throughout contributes to the consensus reached as a consequence of the weights assigned. To rationally retain his personal probability or utility assignment rather than the consensual one requires assigning a weight of zero to others, and that may be inconsistent with his actual evaluation of others. A person who must choose between two consensual assignments need not discount to zero the weights he assigns to either group. He may take some average of the two consensual assignments as his improved probability. Even in the event that he chooses one of the assignments over the other, he is choosing an aggregated probability and not repudiating all aggregated information. It should be noted, of course, that the individual iconoclast may also choose some average of his personal probability assignment and the consensual assignment as his improved assignment. By so doing, however, he is discounting aggregated information and the consequences of it to which he is rationally committed.

The upshot is that one may confront consensual inconsistency. There may be inconsistency between the consensus of one group and that of another. It would be unreasonable to expect a simple formula for resolving such inconsistencies. There is sometimes lattitude for choice even when consensus can be extrapolated from the weights individuals assign. This choice results from conflict and inconsistency. No regimented way of resolving inconsistency

may be available. Confronted with conflict, an individual may find it necessary
to discount to zero at a higher level the evaluations of those he otherwise
respects to escape being committed to a consensus he would find unacceptable. Though the consensual assignment that would result might provide the
most reasonable summary of the total information, a person is not rationally
committed to generating it. He may avoid doing so by assigning zero weight
to others at any level.

13. DIACHRONIC CONSENSUS

So far we have considered the application of the elementary and extended
model at a specific time, or, more accurately, at a specific informational stage.
In the extended model, new information is communicated over a short period
of time through the exchange of anonymous position papers, but it is assumed
that there is no significant external input of information to the group. We
now wish to consider the consequences of new information being obtained
from other sources than simply communication and the changes in consensus
that may result over time. Such consideration reveals the way in which an
individual may, by becoming expert and obtaining the disinterested respect
of others, also become influential in the group. Even if individual probabilities
or utilities are unchanged from time t to time t', changes in consensual assignments at time t and t' may result from a change in the evaluation of members
of the group by each other as we have noted in Chapter Two. For example,
an individual may, at time t, be perceived as a mere neophyte whose judgment
is not to be relied upon very heavily. He may then receive a very small consensual weight, say .000116. If t' is considerably later and he has become a
leader in the interval, then, he may receive a very high weight, say .893. As
a result of this shift, a consensual probability or utility may shift from one
that differs greatly from the individual probability or utility assignment of
the person in question at time t to one that virtually coincides with his assignment at time t'. In fact, there may be a radical shift of this sort with no new
relevant experimental information being obtained in the interval between t
and t'. The shift in the consensual assignment from one time to the next may
result entirely from different consensual weights.

14. INDIVIDUAL AND SOCIETY

Notice that we are still not treating our method as a dynamic method for
changing assignments over time. We are only comparing the synchronic

application of the method at different times. This application of the method is interesting in the following ways. First, it gives us a model for understanding, in a highly ideal fashion, the interaction between the individual and society. At first, an individual can expect to have little impact on social consensus. Thus, his commitment to rational consensus, so far as it is made known to him, will amount to the acceptance of social authority. He may, at this stage, feel that he is committed to conform, which is true, and feel that his opinion is largely discounted by social authority, which is also true. He then has two options. One is to subsequently refuse to grant any positive weight to others, refuse, that is, to aggregate. He thus becomes a temporary iconoclast and may become a permanent one. In the latter case, he becomes a kind of intellectual outlaw, placing himself outside of consensual opinion. He may be forced to conform, but by discounting others to zero, he avoids a rational commitment to the consensus reached by others.

On the other hand, a person who finds that he has little impact on social opinion, who finds that his probabilities, utilities and weights are almost totally discounted by others, may consider what he can do to alter the situation more in his favor. If he were to find that others were disinterested in their evaluation of him, then he might hope to increase his influence on the group by improving his cognitive and social skills. As a result of such improvement, such a person may subsequently obtain the satisfaction of receiving higher consensual weight from others and having greater impact on consensus. Such a person may become a model citizen of the intellectual community, fully committed to the consensus.

Of course, a variety of variations are possible. It should be noted that model citizens may find the strategy of the outlaw tempting when they receive less consensual weight then they expect. This is, we conjecture, most likely to occur when an individual has greatly improved his expertise, and other members of the group have also improved, so that his consensual weight remains virtually the same even when he has become much more highly skilled. In short, there is no guarantee that one will receive greater weight in the aggregation as a result of improving ones skills and knowledge. When accomplishment is not rewarded with greater consensual weight, the individual may feel pressured to conform to social authority that is quite alien to his own views. The strategy of turning outlaw may then have some appeal. One danger of this strategy is that of ostracism. The outlaw, discounting others to zero, will find that they reciprocate. Once this occurs and appears to the individual to be an irreversible process, he may experience the discomfort of having lost even the potential for influencing consensus. Whatever the emotional reaction of the individual to differing strategies, it is an advantage of our model to provide an account of the impact of the individual on society and the society on the individual.

15. SUMMARY AND PROSPECTUS

We have thus presented our model, both in the elementaryy and extended form, with a preliminary mathematical formulation. Both models can, under the appropriate conditions, yield a set of consensual weights that enable us to reach consensual probabilities, utilities, and orderings. The extended model has the advantage of allowing for differential weighting at higher levels and the separation of information applied at those levels. Since one can escape from being driven to consensus by discounting others to zero at any level, we maintain that one who assigns others positive weight generating consensus is rationally committed to the result. We showed how one can deal with questions of iconoclasm, consensual conflict, and the interaction between the individual and society within the extended model. We have thus indicated some applications of our methodology to philosophical problems. In the next chapter, we shall consider further applications of our consensual models to political, ethical, and scientific problems. In subsequent chapters, we shall present the models in mathematical detail, justifying their application axiomatically in Chapter Six. We shall also consider in greater detail in Chapter Seven the formal and methodological issues of assigning weights. Finally, in Chapters Seven and Eight, we elaborate in detail the mathematical conditions for reaching consensus with consensual weights through converging aggregation and the use of a fixed point vector.

CHAPTER FIVE

APPLICATIONS OF THE CONSENSUS MODEL

There are many areas of application for our model of consensus. The most obvious being economic, political, ethical, or all three combined. There are, however, other domains where consensus is germane. Perhaps the two most salient examples are those of science and language. The conception of science is social, science being the activity and product of a group of investigators. What is accepted as science is based on consensus within a scientific community. Again, when we speak of knowledge, of what is known, we implicitly refer to a group and an epistemic consensus within such a group. Finally, when we speak of a language, of the semantics and grammar of language, for example, we describe something communal and, therefore, consensual.

Let us first consider application to the standard problems of social choice in economics, politics and ethics. The problems have, to some extent, already been discussed. It is enlightening, however, to compare our method of social choice to other methodologies. Any method of social choice that excludes the application of relevant information must be judged to be defective. Appeal to preferences alone excludes differential information among the individuals that express those preferences. It is not only that methods based on preferences alone exclude intensity, they also exclude the evaluation of intensity. For example, if one person is judged to have a very intense preferences for a political candidate or for some applicant for a job, the intensity of the preference may be discounted by others on the grounds that the intensity is not well informed, or on the grounds that the person in question always has intense preferences. There is, of course, the old story about the boy who cried wolf. A similar phenomena exists for an individual who has frequently expressed very strong preferences. The intensity of his preference on some important issue is discounted on the grounds that he is overly intense in the articulation of his preferences. People who are passionate about everything have a certain charm, but one is not inclined to reward such charm with the indulgence of every passion. Any theory that ignored intensity of preference would ignore relevant information, and any theory that amalgamated intensity of preference but disregarded the weighting of intensity would also ignore relevant information. The consensual weights we have formulated above articulate and permit us to amalgamate such information.

1. DEMOCRATIC CHOICE

Let us now consider more concrete application of the model to some traditional puzzles. The first is the selection of political candidates, or, in the extreme case, a ruler. Our method may appear anti-democratic. If we select the candidate whose selection has the highest consensual utility, or consensual expected utility, there is no proof that this would yield the same result as a one man, one vote, majoritarian method of selection. However, we suggest that our method is democratic in an extended sense of that term. Each individual is allowed to evaluate the candidate to the best of his ability, as well as to evaluate the evaluators, the evaluator of evaluators, and so on. Each person gets an input, a package vote of utilities, probabilities and weights that represent his information. The output or political choice is the amalgamation of the information people possess. We advocate that decision as a rational and democratic political choice.

There is the objection that one person in the process might strongly influence the choice. This could result when others assign the person in question a very high weight. We think that outcome should be regarded as unobjectionable. However, what if the very high weight that the person receives is a consequence of his own high self-evaluation which others fail to discount? This problem is, in principle, no different from the case in which one evaluates another too generously. This becomes obvious when we impose some restriction on self-evaluation, for example, when we require that each person assign some standard weight to himself. In such a case, a person who wishes to achieve the same result as assigning a high weight to himself might simply assign a disproportionately high weight to someone else with identical or similar views, assuming that such a person exists. Whether a person assigns a disproportionately high weight to himself or another, his assignment fails to fulfill a condition of rationality; it is not a disinterested assignment.

We have noted, as a qualification of our model, that weights and other measures must be assigned in a rational and disinterested manner or else the aggregation of such measures loses the justification which otherwise sustains it. The justification for the model is based on the assumption that the model aggregates the total information of the group. If the weights and other measures are a genuine summary of information, then the requirement that we aggregate total information in making a decision justifies the application of the model. If, on the contrary, the weights represent an egoistic attempt to manipulate social decision making, then it is unacceptable to use those weights as though they were a disinterested summary of information. We insist, therefore, that it is only when the weights are assigned in a disinterested manner and are a summary of genuine information that it is cogent to claim following the method is rational. It could, of course, happen that the method is, in such an imperfect situation, as reasonable as any alternative method, that is, it is no worse than others. But we offer no argument for that conclusion; we concede it would often not be the case.

Our point about simple democracy is, in one way, similar to Plato's argument. Democratic choice based on a simple vote is not, in principle, the best means for selecting a candidate because it is not the best way of aggregating total information. However, it will usually be the case that the best method for selecting a political candidate will not be applicable because people will be motivated by egoism and act dupliciously. Rather than revealing their disinterested opinion, they may present some egoistically motivated measure as their disinterested opinion. Perhaps this is often the case. There is, at any rate, little conviction that others are both willing and able to act in a disinterested political manner, however convinced one is that one is, oneself, able and willing to act in such a manner. Since political action is an arena of suspicious decision making, it is not surprising that an ideal method based on the disinterested summary of information by individuals would often, unfortunately, not be applicable.

The model might still find indirect application in an extended democratic model of political decision making. It is agreed that democratic decision making should, to function for maximal benefit, be informed. If information about candidates is thoroughly exchanged, and if each person also supplies his evaluation of other persons as political experts, as judges of political experts, and so forth, then consensual measures could be elicited. Of course, the same potential problem would arise when people are duplicious in order to influence public opinion. We may, however, offer some justification for democracy in terms of our model when all individuals acquire approximately the same information and thus become equally well informed. In such a situation, one could justify assigning each person equal weight, and, assuming that individual utility scales were unavailable in such a situation, voting would be justified under our method. In short, we regard democracy as being justified by the inability to aggregate information in a rational way in practice. We point out there that there is a better way, in principle, of making political decisions.

It is interesting to note, in this context, that democratic decision making is often thought to rest upon some principle of the moral superiority of that method. For example, some principle of equality might be invoked. It is, however, important to notice that, in some contexts, the principle of equality seems to conflict with empirical fact. If the object of political leadership is to obtain some objective in terms of the governance of people, whether that objective be one of utility or justice, the selection of such leadership rests on estimates of who can bring about that objective most effectively, or, more technically formulated, on which choice gives us a maximal expectation of obtaining such an objective. The question then becomes one of deciding which selection procedure yields the greatest expectation. It seems clear to us that a strategy of amalgamating the total information in a rational manner is such a procedure. Hence, when such an aggregation is possible, it is reasonable, we contend, for such a method to dictate the social choice. We are, moreover, able to justify the democratic aspect of the procedure. Each individual casts what is, in effect, a complex vote, consisting of weights and other summary measures, which yield the outcome. Here the reason for incorporating all of the votes, all of the packages, is that each vote is a package of information. To disregard a vote would be to disregard relevant information. Thus, on our theory, there is a justification for democracy with respect to the input, with respect to the complex vote, to wit, that to deny anyone the voting input is to reject relevant information.

There is another aspect of the voting situation, and hence of democratic procedure, that is clarified by the method. The utilities or preferences of an individual are always relevant information. These utilities or preferences incorporate the evaluation of means and ends. Questions of means are ones that require technical information, or, at least, such information may be germane to the answering of such questions. Consequently, the opinions of some members on the questions of means may be appropriately discounted in the weighting. We take this to be a widely accepted conclusion. With respect to ends, however, it might be doubted whether there is expertise in such matters, and, therefore, the applicability of our method, even under ideal conditions of disinterest and reasonableness, might be questioned.

In moral discussions, it may be alleged that all are equally competent to select the ends and objectives of society. In practice, however, such a perspective rarely dominates behavior. Some people are clearly wiser and more sensible in such matters than others, and their opinions are given appropriately greater weight. There is no actual equality among men in the ability to judge either means or ends. Such individual judgments are subject to evaluation. They are, and should be, given different weight. What is true, however, is that each individual's preferences in such matters are relevant information for the making of policy. That some strange individual prefers to live on a diet of ice cream and vitamin pills and, moreover, prefers that others live in this manner as well, does not commit us to adopting such a policy. But that our society includes an individual with such preferences is a relevant bit of data. The reason it is relevant is that one aim, not the only one, of a society is to allow for the satisfaction of the desires of the individuals in the society. That does not, by any means, commit us to giving equal weight to all such desires. This is plain when we find an individual with destructive desires, for example, that all individuals of some race or religion be destroyed. Different desires should be given different weight. Some, related to justice, should be given compelling weight, others should be given virtually no weight at all. But that a desire exists is a relevant bit of information, to be weighted and evaluated, in the formulation of social policy.

In conclusion, then, our method has the following peculiarity. It explains, we think, the foundations of democratic procedure. When a society has, as one objective, to satisfy the desires of members of that society, then a representation of those desires is relevant information. All relevant information should be amalgamated in any rational decision, time and other resources allowing, and none should be neglected. In so far as a vote is a representation of relevant information, it is clear that no vote can be rationally ignored. On the other hand, in an ideal situation in which the initial votes are a complex package of information about utilities, probabilities and weights, it may turn out that the package supplied by one person will be discounted, that is, the utilities, probabilities and weights assigned by one person may be discounted by others. Again, in the ideal situation, this does not mean that others simply disapprove of assignments that are discounted, but rather that disinterested evaluations, summarizing the information all possess, lead to that result.

Democracy means that each person receives a vote. It also means that others may vote to the contrary. In the latter case, the impact of the first vote may be virtually nullified. Our procedure is a democratic procedure in the sense that each person provides input to the process that yields the outcome. It appears anti-democratic in that the input of one person may receive less weight than that of another. The anti-democratic appearance is illusion. In ordinary voting procedures, the votes cast by those who lose are, in the final outcome, completely discounted anyway. Any loser can, quite properly, remark that the outcome would have been the same if he had not voted at all, and all the losers together can remark collectively that if they had all not voted the outcome would have been exactly the same. The discounting of losing votes in this sense is not an objection to the democracy of a procedure.

The procedure that we have proposed gives each person a vote, and, like the ordinary voting situation, that vote may be discounted in the process of aggregating the votes. In our process, the aggregation is, of course, more complicated than simple counting of votes. However, the complexity is a democratic advantage. Someone who is discounted in one way may be given greater weight in another. Someone whose basic preferences of utilities are given little weight by others may still be highly respected in terms of the probabilities he assigns or in terms of the weights he assigns to others. He may not get his way, but he has had his impact. Thus, according to our method, a person has influence in proportion to the consensually evaluated reliability of his information and evaluations. He can, we suggest, reasonably demand no more. Often no justification for democratic voting procedures are given. It is just postulated that they are fair or reasonable. Our procedure is justified by the commitment to accept the result of rationally aggregating the total information available.

2. JUSTICE AND RIGHTS

The proper application of our theory of consensus enables one to solve a difficult and recalcitrant problem in ethics. The problem arose in the clearest form as an objection to Mill's [1863] act utilitarianism; it is the problem of justice. Simply stated, the problem is that a policy that maximizes some good for society, for example, pleasure or happiness, may treat some one individual with total injustice, for example, by making the individual a scapegoat for a crime to insure the stability of society. There are many such examples, imagined with great vividness by philosophers, and they appear convincing. Closely related to the problem of justice are problems concerning rights discussed, for example, by Feinberg [1974] and Murphy [1979]. When the rights of an individual are abrogated for the social good, he is treated unfairly and with injustice. This is not the appropriate place to explore the complex issues raised by the construction of a theory of justice and rights such as Rawls [1971] and by the critics such as Barry [1973] and Wolff [1977]. However, it is virtue of a theory of social choice that it provides for questions of justice and rights and does not *dictate* the utilitarian choice. Perhaps some form of utilitarianism can accommodate a satisfactory theory of justice and rights. It is our claim that a satisfactory theory of rational social choice should not assume this or the contrary. That is, a theory of social choice should, we propose, allow for either outcome. Information about justice and rights is part of the total information to be amalgamated, and, therefore, a theory of social choice should not presuppose at the outset what that information will tell us.

It is important to reflect briefly on the relation between utilitarianism and justice in order to see very clearly why the problem of justice, as articulated by a variety of authors, cannot be easily solved within a utilitarian framework. It might seem that the scapegoat problem merely reflects some special preferences or utilities attaching to certain kinds of actions people call *just* or *unjust*. Thus, one would think that one could amend traditional hedonistic utilitarian theories associated with Benthan [1789] and Mill [1863], allow that acts of justice are good in themselves, acts of injustice bad in themselves, and proceed as an ideal utilitarian such as Moore [1956]. The utility of justice and injustice would be included in the calculation. To be sure, such a theory would be an improvement, from the standpoint of dealing with issues of justice and injustice, over traditional hedonistic utilitarianism, but the resulting account would, from a certain moral point of view, be defective for the same reason as the original theory. Even if we allow that justice has a very high utility and injustice a very high disutility, still it remains possible, because other goods also have positive utility, that the disutility of injustice could be outweighted by other advantages. Once this is noted, it is clear that attaching utility to justice and disutility to injustice does not solve the problem of the scapegoat: it merely raises the ante on the rightness of unjust acts.

If injustice, such as making some innocent person a scapegoat, has high disutility, then it would take greater other benefits for society to justify the action on utilitarian grounds, but, in principle, there would be no guarantee and unjust action would not turn out to be the right action on utilitarian theory. Some moralists would claim that such a theory is as defective as the original on the grounds that no injustice can ever be morally justified in terms of other benefits to an individual or society. According to such philosophers, one must first provide for justice and, only then, are utilitarian considerations germane. Whether this position is correct or not, it is plausible. A satisfactory theory of social choice should not rule out the possibility of according justice such a special status. Similar remarks apply to the concept of rights.

3. MORALS AND CONSENSUS

How, within our model, can we deal with such concepts as justice and rights? First of all, individuals within a society must be in some way committed to such conceptions, though they may fail, through ignorance or moral obtuseness, to recognize this. The original examples of justice and rights illustrate this. The scapegoat counterexample to utilitarianism is an example of a policy that *we* would judge to be wrong. Similarly, the striking example from Nozick [1974], affirming it would be wrong to remove someone's eyes for the benefit of others, is something we are asked to judge. Another example, one from the lectures of C. J. Ducasse, is the claim that it is wrong to stick pins in babies eyes for our amusement, no matter how amusing we might find this activity. *We* are appealed to with the assurance that *we* will condemn this act. *We* are obviously committed to certain ethical judgments. But it is necessary to explain how we are committed.

It is important to note that not everyone would agree to the observation just made. For example, in some societies it has been thought right to blind someone for the sake of society, for example, if the person is prone to commit some crime, perhaps has done so repeatedly, and the deprivation of vision is deemed an appropriate means of punishment and prevention of subsequent recurrence. This might be, for example, a punishment for looking upon some object, a holy object perhaps, when such observation is prohibited, or, in a particularly puritanical society, for acts of voyeurism. *We* may judge such retribution to be unjust and, perhaps, a violation of rights, but those in another society might hold utterly different principles on the matter. Even the case of the scapegoat is subject to such observation. In a society that believes in the existence of angry gods who must, on occasion, be appeased by human sacrifice, the selection of a completely innocent person as a sacrifice, perhaps because only such a sacrifice is believed to be efficacious, is not dissimilar to the example of the scapegoat. In some societies such an action might be regarded as neither a violation of rights nor injustice. Of course, *we* regard those actions as both injustice and a violation of the rights of the individual. The problem is to find some foundation for these judgments.

4. DISCOUNTING UNJUST UTILITIES

As we have noted, utilitarian theories, though they assign high utility to justice and the upholding of rights, cannot guarantee that the disutility of injustice and the violation of rights will not be overridden by the utility of some other good. Our consensual theory, because it applies weights in addition to utilities, allows the possibility of excluding from consideration any utility function, any utility evaluation, allowing for other benefits to override the application of justice and the upholding of rights. The mechanism by which these results may be excluded is simple enough to formulate. We need only require that utility assignments that override justice or rights be discounted to zero. If we assign a weight of zero to the utility assignment of a person with respect to any action in which that person assigns utilities in such a way that an injust action, treating someone as a scapegoat for example, has greater utility than any just alternative, then we indicate, thereby, our unwillingness to countenance such a utility assignment for the purpose of moral deliberation.

Some individuals might evaluate actions that are injust or violate rights as having greater utility, but *we* consider such evaluations to constitute the sort of error in evaluation that warrants our discounting such evaluations completely. The case is similar in some respects to that in which we conclude that some scientist performs certain experiments in a defective manner. We might then discount to zero the information he supplies, in this case his probability assignment pertaining to these matters, because of his faulty procedure. For example, if we discovered that the experimenter wrote down the results of the experiments before he conducted them and sometimes failed to alter his report subsequently, we might discount his experimental judgments completely. The problem in both cases would be that someone has violated a rule that must be satisfied before evaluations are to be taken seriously.

Suppose, then, that in accordance with our proposal, everyone discounts to zero those members of society who assign utilities in such a way that injust action, or an action that violates rights, has greater utility or expected utility than others that do not. What is the result? It is that the utility assignment of such a person will receive zero consensual weight, and his assignment will have no influence upon the consensual utility assignment. In effect, this amounts to a decision not to amalgamate whatever information he possesses into the consensual decision. Like the case of the defective experimenter, we might concede that there is a mixture of information and error reflected in his utility assignment, but, since he has violated a basic constraint on method or procedure required in this domain, we must discount his assignment completely.

The foregoing reflections show that we may, if we consider it reasonable, discount certain utility assignments to zero and thus insure that no utility assignment we judge to sustain injustice or the violation of rights receives any weight at all in the consensual utility assignment. We treat such assignments as though they rest upon error and, therefore, do not contain information to be amalgamated. It is worth noting, however, that there is less than universal agreement, even among sensitive and intelligent people, about the exact status of justice and rights. Some conceive of rights, for example, as merely *prima facie* restrictions that may be overriden in some cases. We choose not to take sides in this dispute. Even scapegoat or sacrifice cases can be made more perplexing. If we imagine a case in which some maniac controls a device that, if fired by him, would destroy the whole human race, and he demands an innocent sacrifice as a condition of defusing the device, perhaps agreeing to set things up in such a way that if the required sacrifice is made then the device will be automatically defused, it is not perfectly clear to all that it would be wrong to provide such a sacrifice. We do not defend this judgment, and we agree that it would be manifestly injust and unfair to the innocent selected, it would violate the rights of such a person, but when the entire human race is at stake, when our extermination is virtually certain otherwise, perhaps some might think that considerations of rights and justice can be overridden. It is, we suggest, an advantage of our theory that, though it allows for the extreme view that justice and rights cannot, in principle, be out-weighted by other benefits, it also allows for the other point of view. We may, in some extreme cases, wish to give some weight, perhaps small, to utility assignments that allow for other considerations to override those of justice and rights. What we think desirable about the consensual theory of rationality in application to such cases is that it allows for the extreme view in these matters, but it does not *mandate* such a position. Thus, the consensual theory permits us to explain how such results might be achieved, how they could be articulated within a theory of rationality, without thereby laying them down as constraints on such a theory.

5. MORALITY AND RATIONALITY

It is perhaps worth reflecting briefly on the relation between morality and rationality in this context. We think that it is an open question whether every moral action is rational. Some philosophers have attempted to identify the moral choice with the rational choice, all things considered. Others demure. There appear to be arenas of human choice whether morals do not determine the choice, for example in the choice of different flavors of ice cream. It might be irrational for me to choose a flavor I found offensive, licorice for example, though there would be nothing immoral in such a choice. Thus, rational choice has a wider domain than moral choice. The question, however, is whether there can be actions that are immoral but still rational. There may be some inclination to view the case of the maniac described above in this way. It might be regarded as immoral to supply an innocent sacrifice to the maniac, but it might, at the same time, be regarded as the rational thing to do. If one allows such a possibility, and we neither advocate nor oppose such a conception here, then one might wish to say that the consensual, the socially rational, need not necessarily coincide with the moral. In that case, though we would continue to advocate our method as supplying the consensually rational choice, we would not claim such a choice to be the consensually moral one. It should be noted, however, that it would be possible to apply our method to obtain the consensually moral choice. One would need to restrict utility functions to those that represent *purely moral* considerations and then aggregate. Thus, the methodology cannot be assumed to always yield the morally consensual choice, but application can be restricted to guarantee that result.

The important consequence of applying the method in the moral domain, as we indicated above, is that it provides us with a justification for following the consensual directive. Kant [1785] spoke about the respect for individuals as ends in themselves. We contend that one aspect of such respect is the respect accorded to individuals as rational and moral agents. We may, in some circumstances, for one reason or another, give no positive weight to the utility assignments or to the moral evaluations of another. That is, we suggest, an extreme situation. However, when we do respect others and assign a positive weight to their evaluations, we are bound by consistency to accept the consequences of that respect. That means, with the qualifications discussed in earlier chapter, we are committed to the consensually moral or rational position.

Thus, we can see how the method forms the foundation for moral and rational decision making. If a group is unified by the communication of positive respect so that aggregation converges toward a consensual assignment, then the members are, with certain given qualifications, committed to the outcome. Thus, a group assigning zero respect at some level to individuals, for example, those who have utility assignments that would warrant injustice or the violation of rights, may elicit reciprocal discounting from those individuals at the next level. Individuals receive respect from others in a community ordinarily, and when they receive no such respect, they may regard themselves as excluded from membership in the community. In such instances, those receiving no respect may also refuse to give respect and thus do not participate in the consensual outcome. Therefore, they are uncommitted to the resulting consensus. The larger group may then decompose into smaller groups, each of which contains members who communicate respect to each other and, therefore, have a consensus. But the larger group has no consensus. It seems to us that this is some argument against assigning zero weight to the utility assignments of others, and, therefore, some argument against holding the extreme view on justice and rights requiring complete discounting of utility assignments of those who think that injustice and the violation of rights can, in extreme cases, be outweighed by other benefits. We concede, however, this consideration might itself be outweighed by some argument on behalf of such moral conceptions. We simply note the disadvantage of discounting altogether any utility assignment of another. Such discounting brings with it the threat of social decomposition, and, therefore, the impossibility of aggregating the total information in rational decision making.

6. MORAL RELATIVISM

The question of the decomposition of groups into moral subsocieties brings with it the perennial question of moral relativism. If there is within each of two groups a moral consensus, but the two groups conflict with each other, must we admit that each group is equally reasonable? Our theory by no means mandates such a conclusion. If one considers the two groups as a disinterested outsider, one might note the consensus within each groups was arrived at in a formally identical manner, and, on formal grounds alone, there are no grounds for choosing between them. However, one is rarely such an observer. When, in fact, a person makes judgments in moral matters, usually he belongs to one group, a group in which he communicates respect to others and receives such respect. If I am such a person, then, when I look at some alternative group, where I neither give nor receive respect, I am in no way neutral between the two groups. On the contrary, though I concede that both groups reached consensus in a formally similar way, I may regard the consensus of the other group as an aggregation of ignorance, that is why I assign zero weight to the members of that group initially and completely discount their claims to knowledge. On the other hand, I regard the consensus of my own group as the aggregation of information. Thus, I can be expected to advocate the consensus to which I contribute and reject the consensus I discounted originally. The fact that both groups proceed in *formally* identical ways to aggregate their opinions and evaluations does not, in any way, show that their original opinions and evaluations were equally meritorious.

The method of aggregation is not a method for deciding between the consensual opinions and evaluations of different groups. We do not, however, deny that there may be such methods. Neither do we affirm that there must be. The question of what the best methods are for making personal judgments is not one we have sought to answer here. We have, instead, advocated a method for amalgamating such judgments and thereby obtaining interpersonal judgments. The ultimate reliability of the output depends on the initial reliability of the input. Thus, neither relativism nor refutation of relativism is a consequence of accepting and applying our model of consensual rationality in ethics and morals.

7. SCIENCE AND CONSENSUS

In Chapter Two, we have discussed the application of the consensus model to scientific acceptance. It is important, however, to review these results in a wider context of epistemology and philosophy of science in order to understand why the concept of consensus should be accorded a central role. The importance derives from the failure of Cartesian epistemology to provide the foundations of science. This theory told us that science should begin with certain and indubitable propositions, ones clear and self-evident, and hence free from any chance of error. The theory was intended to rid us of all false assumptions or doubtful premises thereby founding science on the bedrock of certainty. This theory retains some vitality, but, in general, it is discredited. The reason is that such a restriction of what is certain as evidence will lead us to an acute form of skepticism. We shall, if so constrained, be forced to throw out the corpus of scientific knowledge as mere conjecture and illusion. The basic observation reports, those that formulate the results of experiment and controlled observation, are, though reliable for scientific purposes, by no means certain. It is clear that such reports may contain errors, and, as a matter of historical fact, have been erroneous. Science is not and cannot be founded on certainty.

In science, we always have a choice when theoretical formulation confronts empirical articulation of rejecting one or the other. Whatever choice we make, we require some rational basis for our decision. We may reject the theoretical claim when it conflicts with the report of observation, but that is not our only alternative. We may, instead, retain the theory and reject the observation report as erroneous. Or, we may even reject those statements that render the theoretical formulations inconsistent with the observation reports. When confronting such a choice and seeking to proceed rationally, we must reflect upon the chances of obtaining the truth and avoiding error under each choice. Such reflection, to be rational, must be based on the total information available, for example, on the probability assignment summarizing such information. That means, of course, the consensual probability assignment when it aggregates such information. We are here indebted to Sellars [1974].

8. COGNITIVE DECISION MAKING

Some clarification of this argument is essential. It is clear that the acceptance or rejection of some hypothesis or theory in science, for example, the hypothesis that the sun is round, is a cognitive or intellectual decision. There is a traditional conception of rational scientific method pertaining to such decisions, and, crudely formulated, it is the hypothetico-deductive method. The central idea is that from a theory one deduces observation consequence O, and the decision of whether to accept or reject the theory T is determined by ascertainment of the truth of observation consequence O. This delightfully simple picture of scientific decision making is, however, most inadequate.

This is noted when one considers the conflict between falsificationist conceptions of science, Popper [1963] being the most illustrious defender, and confirmation or inductivist views of science. The former assert that the hypothetical-deductive method is really a method of rejection by test, a theory being rejected when the observation consequence is falsified by empirical test and otherwise retained. The confirmation or inductivist views claim that a theory can be confirmed or inductively supported by empirical test instead of being falsified. Within this group, we find conflict over the question of whether confirmation or support is to be interpreted as probability, Carnap [1962] being the most notable advocate, or as some other relation, as Cohen [1976] contends. Moreover, there are then a wide group of philosophers, Hempel [1962], Levi [1967], Hintikka and Pietarinen [1966], Hilpinen [1968], and Lehrer [1974] included, who have argued that the decision of whether to accept or reject theories and hypotheses in science should be construed as a rational decision problem on the analogy of practical decision problems. Finally, a subgroup, Lehrer [1974] and Levi [1968], have noted that the decision to accept some statement as evidence, for example, a report of the outcome of an empirical test, is also a decision to be considered on the same model. Thus, the simplicity of the hypothetico-deductive method vanishes in the complexity of interpretation.

The best way to clarify the point is to view the matter schematically. Suppose we have theory T and attempt to deduce some empirical consequence O. It has been noted that, in addition to the purely theoretical conceptions of T, we require some connecting or interpreting sentences C relating theory to observation in order to effect the deduction of O. Now suppose that some empirical test leads us to think that O is false. One might be inclined to conclude, therefore, that theory T must be rejected. Notice, however, that instead of rejecting T, we might reject the connecting sentences C, thus retaining T.

perhaps together with some new connecting sentences C' disallowing the deduction of O. We have yet another possibility, one not often noticed, which is to decide to retain both T and C but refuse to repudiate O in spite of the empirical test. Our test results are always subject to error, and science students prudently follow the practice of rejecting their experimental results when they conflict with some well established scientific theory. Thus, the choice of which sentences to accept or reject, whether theoretical, connecting or observational, involves some risk of error. Decision making under risk is based on probabilities and utilities, according to standard decision theoretic models. Moreover, refusal to accept a theory and connecting sentences together with the negation of some deduced observation sentence reveals a preference for logical consistency. This preference is in turn justified by the objective of avoiding error. When the set of sentences one accepts is logically inconsistent, error becomes a certainty.

Thus, the decision or choice one makes in scientific activity cannot disregard the risk or chance of error. When a scientist says that a theory has been experimentally falsified, he actually advocates a rather complex decision to accept certain observation sentences describing what is observed, to also accept certain connecting sentences permitting the derivation of the negation of the observation sentences accepted, and, therefore, in the interests of consistency and the avoidance of error, to reject the theory used in the derivation. Similarly, when a philosopher says that a theory is confirmed by observation, he advocates a complex decision to accept certain observation sentences and certain probability relations, or some other relations of inductive support, yielding the result that the theory together with connecting sentences is probable or inductively supported.

It is here important to notice that the acceptance of probability relations is a basic assumption. As is familiar to those who work in probability theory, when '$p(A/B)$' is the probability of A on B, the following probability relations hold:

$$p(T\&C/O) = \frac{p(O/T\&C)p(T\&C)}{p(O)}$$

But it is clear that for any theory T and connecting sentence C such that the expectation of O being true is high on the assumption of their joint truth, that is, $p(O/T\&C)$ is high, we can construct some competing theory T' and connecting sentences C' that yield the same expectation to the same degree. Skeptical arguments often contain the formulation of such competing theories, for example, Descartes' evil demon hypothesis. This means that if we assume that the probability of (*T* and *C*) is higher than the conjunction of competing theories and connecting sentences, it is because we assign a higher probability to (*T* and *C*) initially. We obtain the higher conditional probability of *T* and *C* on *O* as a result.

The upshot is that decision making in science is decision making under risk, such decision making is based on probabilities, and those probabilities, in turn, are based on prior antecedent or unconditional probabilities of theories and their connecting sentences. To decide what it is rational to accept, therefore, we must have some method for assigning prior probabilities, the probability of (*T* and *C*) for example. The latter assignment of probabilities must itself be rational. We propose that a rational assignment should amalgamate the available information, and, therefore, our consensual theory is suitable to supply such probabilities. It should be noted that some philosophers, Jeffrey [1970] and Carnap [1962] for example, have had their doubts about the notion of accepting or rejecting theories, hypotheses and other sentences. According to this group of philosophers, who may be called extreme probabilists, it suffices to assign probabilities. However, according to such philosophers, we must have some way of assigning initial or unconditional probabilities, especially those probabilities assigned to reports of observation. So, even for such an extreme probabilist position, it is necessary to have a methodology for assigning these probabilities.

We may formulate the preceding points with greater decision theoretic precision. When a person seeks to obtain truth and avoid error, he must seek to obtain maximal or at least positive expected utility measured in terms of those objectives. Thus, if a scientist deliberates about whether to accept some sentence *S*, he must contemplate at least two outcomes, that he thus accepts what is true and that he thus accepts what is false. He must then consider the probability of obtaining each outcome, that is, $p(S)$ and $p(-S)$, as well as the value of obtaining each outcome. Letting '$e(S)$' be the expected utility, '$u_t(S)$' be the utility of accepting *S* when it is true, and '$u_f(S)$' be the utility of accepting *S* when it is false, we obtain the following equation:

$$e(S) = p(S)u_t(S) + p(-S)u_f(S).$$

The expected utility is the sum of the products of the probability of getting each outcome times the utility measured in terms of seeking truth and the avoiding of error. Of course, this formula is subject to many variations and modifications. One may, once one has accepted a sentence as evidence, consider the conditional probabilities and utilities on such evidence. Moreover, it is left open by the formula how we are to define utilities. What remains clear and central, however, is that the ascertainment of probabilities in a rational manner remains fundamental. Lehrer [1974, 1976] has suggested that utilities may, together with semantic notions, be defined in terms of probabilities as well. Whether this proposal satisfactorily articulates the utilities or not, probability remains salient and fundamental for the ascertainment of rational decision making.

9. CONSENSUAL AND SUBJECTIVE PROBABILITIES

We shall conclude this section with a few words on our reason for thinking that consensual probabilities are superior to other probability assignments for the purposes of rational decision making in science and other cognitive enterprises. Basically, the reason is that other conceptions of probability are either idiosyncratic, inadequate to articulate all the information available, or simply insufficient. Simple subjectivist measures, discussed above, are clearly too idiosyncratic. Different scientists will be expected to make different personal probability assignments to the same hypotheses, theories and experimental reports. This should be expected even when, in the sense articulated, the scientists accept the same hypotheses, theories and experimental reports. Whether they agree in what they accept on the basis of personal probability assignments or not, it would be surprising indeed if they assigned exactly the same probabilities. Since differences are to be expected, it is important to have some method for amalgamating the diverse information contained in and summarized by the personal probability assignments of various scientists and investigators.

The foregoing considerations are especially important when one considers that science is fundamentally a social enterprise. There is a division of labor within the field that is quite essential to scientific articulation. At the most obvious level, investigators may supply *different* experimental evidence from their research. Such evidence, reflected in personal probability assignments, must be aggregated. Moreover, one standard methodology for amalgamating such information, that of merely assigning all alleged evidence statements a probability of one, is clearly defective and unrealistic. The person who reports on his experimental findings may, if he is not philosophically self-critical, assign a probability of one to the statements articulating his results. It is historically obvious, however, that such statements are sometimes erroneous and should be assigned a probability less than unity to reflect the risk of error in even the most painstaking experimental reporting. In fact, the experimental results of an investigator will be subject to scrutiny and evaluation by other scientists before they are amalgamated into science, or included within the corpus of scientific knowledge. Thus, science does not proceed by the immediate unreflective incorporation of experimental reports. Instead, such reports are weighed and evaluated. Whether they are accepted depends, therefore, upon the evaluation of their reliability. Our method provides a consensual evaluation in terms of consensual weights for probabilities permitting us to incorporate experimental results into scientific knowledge in a rational manner.

It should be noted that such evaluation is not, of course, limited to experimental reports, to the articulation of data. When a scientist presents or defends some theory or hypothesis, this must also be evaluated before being accepted or rejected. The evaluation does not consist, moreover, in some simple matching of the theory or hypothesis to the data. There will always be logically competing theories and hypotheses that contradict each other but are compaticle with the empirical results so far gathered. Indeed, arguments from Duhem [1954] and Quine [1960] lead to the conclusion that there will *always* exist such competing theories consistent with the empirical results, no matter how complete those results may be. The reason is simply that empirical data must, inevitably, underdetermine theory. It is easy to appreciate this fact in terms of the schematic account we formulate above. If we need connecting statements C in order to connect theory T to observation consequences O, it seems clear enough that we can construct a theory logically incompatible with T, say T', which when combined with the appropriate connecting sentences will also enable us to deduce the same observation consequences O. The consequence, therefore, is that considerations other than the evidence will inevitably influence the acceptance or rejection of a theory in science. This point is, of course, simply a reinforcement of the point made above that the probability assignment of a theory on evidence will be strongly influenced by the assignment of prior probabilities to the theory.

With the strictly personalist or subjective framework, therefore, theories and hypotheses will be assigned probabilities on the basis of evidence, but, assuming that those probabilities are strongly influenced by prior or antecedent probabilities, they can be expected to vary from individual to individual. Thought experiments, considerations of simplicity and coherence with other theories, can be expected to have their differential impact on the individual probability assignments. We then require some method for evaluating these diverse sources of information and amalgamating the information into the body of science. Therefore, a subjectivist or personalist theory of probability must be supplemented by a method for amalgamating the probability assign-ments of various individuals, and this is what our consensual model accom-plishes.

10. STATISTICAL PROBABILITIES

The next kind of probability statements sometimes alleged to serve as the basis of scientific epistemology are statistical. Various interpretations of statistical probability statements have been provided, but our objection to relying solely on such statements to articulate the epistemological basis of accepting or rejecting statements into the body of science is directed toward the method for determining statistical probability statements, however they may then be precisely interpreted. One fundamental method of such theories is inference from what is observed in a sample to a probability statement of the kind in question. What is required is that one infer probabilities from the percentages counted in a sample as in Reichenbach [1949]. If one counts in a sample of 10,000 that 6510 have some quality Q the others lack, it is this information that determines the probabilities, perhaps together with other information of the same sort. We do not object to such theories of prob-ability. We do doubt that they are adequate to give us a theory of the rational acceptance or rejection of statements in science. The reason for our skepticism is that the information in a sample is restricted to what is regimented in a special way, that is, to what is counted.

Moreover, the rational acceptence of statements about the sample itself already presupposes a probability assignment. The point has already been made above in discussion of the personalist theory. When a scientist considers a sample and decides a member of the sample has a specific property, for example, when he looks through a microscope and decides that a cell is damaged, the decision already involves some risk of error. Since it is a deci-sion under risk, the probability of error must be considered if the decision is a rational one. There are general mathematical considerations from the theory of errors that can be brought to bear on this matter, but there are also other relevant considerations, the reliability of the microscope and the reliability of microscopist for example. Pure mathematics does not supply the answer to these questions. Moreover, it is very unlikely that the investigator himself will have any statistical data to supply him with the probabilities. He will almost surely not have counted his successes and failures in the past, though he will almost surely have less regimented information germane to such ques-tions. And, of course, the same will be true of others faced with the question of how much weight to give to his results. Thus, the problem of the statistical theory, most simply put, is that there is more information available to us than counting samples.

The same problem emerges again when we have decided what we have observed in the sample. For we may have other information, in addition to the results observed in a sample, that we shall wish to take into consideration when deciding what probabilities to assign. This is especially obvious in the case of theories and hypotheses where we must weigh considerations of simplicity, coherence and so forth. For here surely we lack statistical data concerning the success or failure of theories obtained from the consideration of samples. Again, there is more information available to us than what has been counted in samples. The precept to restrict our scientific decision making to what has been inferred from samples presupposes other probabilities in order to enable us to rationally decide what reports about the samples to accept. Moreover, it excludes us from considering relevant information. Thus, statistical methodology, though important in science, cannot provide us with the epistemological foundations of science. To use all information available to us, we must go beyond what we have counted to amalgamate the diverse information possessed by different individuals.

11. LOGICAL PROBABILITIES

Finally, there are logical or semantic theories of probability. Carnap [1962] and Hintikka [1966] have formulated such theories. As both of them have indicated, most strikingly Hintikka, there is an enormous range of possible probability assignments permitted by such a methodology. Our proposal, therefore, is that such logical or semantic probability assignments be regarded as simply limiting the range of coherent probability assignments. The choice from within such a set of possibilities remains open and, we propose, should be decided in the light of the information available. Our consensual method may be used to select a probability assignment on the basis of aggregated information.

We have, so far, advocated the application of our method to science within a probabilistic or Bayesian framework. The application of our methodology is, however, by no means limited to such a framework. We noted earlier that our method may be used to find consensual weights to be assigned to members of a community. These consensual weights may then be used to make a choice in science on the basis of other measures than probabilities. Measures of corroboration or inductive support may also be amalgamated. A similar point about the distribution of information would again be appropriate. All such measures depend on a base of empirical information, and different individuals, having different information, may be expected to differ in the values they assign by such measures. Thus, once again, we confront the problem of needing to aggregate diverse information. Moreover, even when a decision is to accept or reject something other than a statement, for example, to accept some experimental method, technique of theoretical extrapolation, paradigm or procedure, our model is again suitable. The consensual weight assigned to some individual or subgroup of individuals may establish scientific leadership and rational dominance within some area of science. Their views and methods may thus become canons or principles of scientific procedure that guide the enterprise. When leadership is selected from a rational amalgamation of information concerning respect and reliability, the selection is rational rather than subversive with respect to the goals of scientific inquiry.

We note, therefore, that science, being a communal activity, must have some method for pooling the contributions of individuals of the scientific community with an end to scientific decision making. Scientific knowledge is ideally a social product aggregating information distributed among scientists. As an ideal, it is, perhaps, a normative fiction. We propose our model as the fulfillment of a normative ideal of the rational aggregation of scientific information. We note that practise, though influenced by the ideal, involves less rational procedures.

12. LANGUAGE AND CONSENSUS

It is now useful to consider the application of our method of consensus to the communal aspects of language. We may think of a speaker as possessing his idiolect, and in this idiolect he refers to objects and means something by what he says. In a special situation, a speaker and hearer may share a dialect, perhaps because they are siblings, and they may prefer their dialect to the communal language. There will, in fact, be sublanguages within the shared languages that differ from the communal language. However, individuals participate in a communal language, and the problem is how to explicate the relations between individuals that combine individual speakers and listeners into a language community.

It is jejune to remarks that a communal language rests on some convention or consensus. One way to attempt to explicate this is in terms of the model of nested expectations of Lewis [1969], Grice [1969] and Shiffer [1972]. The motivations for speech are multiple and complex, and the problem of the speaker is to maximize his expectation of achieving his multiple and crossed purposes. He must, to that end, know what he values, and he must adjust his expectations to his convictions about the expectations of his prospective listener. This listener, in turn, confronts the speaker with his purposes and expectations, among those being his beliefs about the expectations of the speaker, about the expectations of the speaker about his expectations, and so forth. Such patterns of expectation do not, however, give us a complete account. In the first place, it would need to be supplemented with an explanation of how people can differ in their expectations, as they surely do, and yet have a consensus sufficient for the postulation of a public language. Secondly, some individuals in a society, in a language community, are assigned greater linguistic authority in some domains then others. If the more authoritative individuals fail to fulfill the expectations of others, or the expectations of others about the expectations the experts have about the expectations of others, that does not, in any way, threaten the consensus upon which language rests. The simple reason is that, with respect to some words, we delegate our authority to others, and when they do not fulfill our expectations about language use, we conclude that they are correct and accept their usage.

Putnam [1973] has made this point very clearly. As he puts the matter, there is a division of labor within the language community that assigns authoritative decision making over some aspect of language to specific groups of individuals. The most obvious example is, of course, scientific language. A simple example is the use of the word 'molecule.' Most of us use this word in more or less ordinary parlance to refer to microscopic bits of matter that are collections of atoms that compose certain familiar substances. When we see a crystal lying upon a table, quite visible to the naked eye, we would not call it a molecule. When a scientist tells us that this is but a single molecule, we are amazed, but, if we are convinced of his scientific reliability, we will, of course, agree that the object is a molecule. This sort of example is important because it is relevant to both meaning and reference. It is clear from the example that the usual expectations about what the word 'molecule' would be used to refer to are violated. So the referential use of the word does not fulfill our expectations. It is also clear that the reason our expectations about reference are not fulfilled in that our expectations concerning the semantic use of the word are not satisfied. We expect other speakers to use the word 'molecule' so that part of the meaning of the word is that a molecule is microscopic, and this expectation is thwarted by the scientist in question. The size of the molecule exceeds our semantic expectations.

13. LINGUISTIC INDETERMINACY

The preceding example indicates that our consensus about the meaning and reference of words in a language is, in one sense, a fiction. It is, in fact, not necessary that agreement be very great, providing that we have agreement about how to resolve disagreement. Sometimes this involves reference to authorities, sometimes appeal to examplars, and there are, in fact, other strategies for resolving dissensus as well. One ideal strategy for finding the required consensus beneath the surface of disagreement would be to aggregate total information according to our model. To accomplish this, it is first neces- sary to note that the usual treatment of reference and semantics overlooks indeterminacy of reference and meaning. It is common practise in philosophy, and among prominent linguists, to consult intuition to obtain a prompt an- swer to the question of whether some condition is included in the meaning of a word. The answer to such questions must be either yes or no, and the results are then assumed to be valid for the language. There is a certain prescientific charm to such a procedure, and it is certainly far less work than more exact investigation of the speakers within a language community. It is not too dif- ficult to see the defect in such a procedure. It is that individuals disagree in the answers they pose to such questions, and, indeed, the honest individual will quickly note that he has varying degrees of uncertainty in such matters. Empirical research, for example by A. Lehrer [1974], establishes the fact of such variation. The assumption of agreement is, in fact, science fiction.

An example taken from A. Lehrer [1974] may illustrate the point. Sup- pose we ask subjects whether an object that is not made of metal can be correctly described as a 'can', and suppose we ask them to indicate how cer- tain they are about the correctness of their answer. There will be those who think it is certainly incorrect, those who are less certain, and so forth. This sort of result can be thought of as either a result concerning meaning or reference, as result concerning whether 'can' semantically implies 'made of metal' or whether 'can' refers to objects that are not made of metal. In either case, the answers to the question will represent varying degrees of uncertainty about the relation in question. Relations of uncertainty are, in recent philo- sophical discourse, thought of as probability relations. Thus, I propose that we think of semantic relations as a special form of probability relations. These are probability relations that correspond to the sort of probability relations Carnap sought to develop. According to Carnap [1962], we have probability relations that represent only semantic information. From these original prob- ability relations together with factual information, we obtain other measures which represent the combination of semantic relations and empirical data. We may adopt this conception of probability to our purposes by thinking of some probability relations as holding in every possible world, thus as being independent of the factual nature of that world, and other probability measures as blending semantic and empirical information.

Jeffrey [1965], advocating a method for shifting probabilities in the confrontation with empirical data, suggests holding conditional probabilities constant on grounds that they may be thought of as representing semantic relations. Skyrms [1980] has then showed that this methodology is equivalent to certain assumption about higher level probabilities. If we assume that it is acceptable to speak of the probabilities of probabilities, then it seems natural to presuppose that certain probabilities, perhaps some conditional probabilities, are ones that are themselves assigned a probability of unity. That probability is not diminished by empirical information. Whatever the world is like, the probability relation in question holds. These remarks will seem controversial to some, perhaps obscure to others, and this is not the appropriate place to defend a theory of higher order probability. Moreover, it may be the case that the indeterminacy we are concerned with may better be represented in terms of some other metric or nonmetrical ranking. We assume here that the relations of meaning and reference may be represented in an idealized way as probability relations. These probability relations, unlike empirical probabilities, are the probabilities assigned by a speaker at a time in the actual world, and they are assumed by the speaker to hold for all possible worlds.

For example, if a person assigns a *semantic* probability of .7 to the statement that something is not a can conditional on the statement that is not made of metal, $p(-C/-M) = .7$, this means that this probability assignment is independent of what the world is like, and, more specifically, of the frequency with which many things of certain shape, use and composition occur. A person who thought it was clearly contradictory to say that something that was not metal was, nevertheless, a can, would assign a probability of one, that is, for him $p(-C/-M) = 1$. On our theory, therefore, we have a set of semantically determined probability values, where the values 1 and 0 are simply extreme assignments. There are many further refinements of these matters that one can envisage, but it is our objective here simply to sketch an ideal theory.

14. LINGUISTIC DIVERSITY

People may be expected to disagree in the semantic probabilities they assign. This means, therefore, that the problem of explicating in what sense we have a communal language appears to be more difficult than originally supposed. When we suppose that relations of meaning and reference are nonquantitative, then the variety of diverse opinions is limited to the opinion that the relation in question holds or does not hold. Once we introduce probability relations, however, the possibilities are infinitely greater. It is clear that there is this greater diversity and, therefore, that nonquantitative models fail to articulate the variety which actually exists.

How, then, are we to explain the existence of a communal language, of consensus over such matters, when, in fact, diversity is the rule? The answer is that diversity in idiolects is harmless, both for communication and for scientific description, so long as we know how to resolve our differences when the need arises. The fiction that we all agree, when in fact we do not, is harmless enough providing we are committed to some method or procedure for resolving our differences when they matter. Empirical studies, again those of A. Lehrer [1975], indicate that people find discussion perfectly satisfactory when there is very little referential agreement, for example, when they discuss the wine they imbibe. Here the need for referential exactitude and rectitude is minimal, and the ficton of agreement suffices for all to drink and speak amiably. Discussion about the history of philosophy among philosophers often has a similar flavor. Referential accuracy is not always essential for the satisfactions of linguistic intercourse.

We have, however, the fiction of a consensus. We conceive of a language, English for example, as a linguistic edifice unified by consensus and agreement. Let us concede that quite often the actual dissensus among language users creates no difficulty. Two fundamental questions remain. The first is — how we are to find consensus when it is needed to resolve disagreement? Secondly, if the member of a speech community do not actually agree, how· must they be related in order to constitute such a community?˙ To answer both of these questions, we need a more exact conception of the fiction that is our communal language.

15. LINGUISTIC AUTHORITY AND CONSENSUS

To answer the foregoing questions, let us reconsider the point derived from Putnam [1973] that says that language involves a division of labor. This is another way of saying that decision making authority concerning language usage is not uniformly distributed throughout the community. It is distributed, instead, unevenly depending on the respect and status accorded individuals in certain domains of linguistic usage. In effect, authority is often delegated, directly or indirectly, from some members of a speech community to others. Our contention is that if we understand this process or relation we shall be able to answer the two questions raised above. For once we designate certain individuals as authorities in a linguistic domain, we may appeal to them to resolve disputes. The relations that connect us to each other in such a way as to distribute linguistic authority are, moreover, precisely those that are constitutive of a speech community.

A fundamental relation is one of respect for another, of giving positive weight to him and what he says. Without such respect, we have no community, and, therefore, no communal language. We may remain an aggregation of individuals, perhaps with similar idiolects, but with no means of deciding linguistic questions for the speakers belonging to the aggregate. This respect for others is not merely respect for linguistic competence, it is respect for them as people who understand what they say. We require indirect chains of respect to connect many speakers to those who are most expert. Most people, for example, do not know many of those who are expert in a scientific field, but, nevertheless, authority is delegated to such experts by the linguistic community for the use of words imbedded in the theories and hypotheses of the science in question.

According to our consensual model, such authority is delegated through a chain of respect of the following sort. We start from a person p_1, who gives positive weight to person p_2, who gives positive weight to person p_3, and so on to person p_n who is expert in the field. Note that person p_1 may not give positive weight to any of the people p_j, where j is greater than 2, because person p_1 may be ignorant of the competence of those individuals. For a chain of respect to exist, it is necessary, in principle, that each person in the chain assign positive respect to the next person, but it is not necessary that any more positive respect than that be given. These chains of positive respect bind the individual members together into a speech community. According to our method for aggregating such respect, we may obtain consensual weights for individuals in the community. These weights summarize the information contained in a community about the expertise and special linguistic competence of members of the community. They may be used to average individual semantic probabilities to find a consensual semantic probability assignment.

16. LINGUISTIC CORRECTNESS

Our aggregation procedure gives us a normative model of consensus in a speech community. It is clear that questions of language often have a normative flavor. For example, one speaks of certain forms of speech as being *correct* and others as *incorrect*, some as *right* others as *wrong*. There is no need, I believe, to insist on such an obvious fact. If someone in his idiolect uses the word 'molecule' so that the meaning of the word yields the consequence that it applies only to microscopic objects, then his use of the word is incorrect in English. Similarly, if someone uses the word 'fish' so as to include whales, then he does not use the word correctly from the standpoint of English usage. These are scientific examples, but there are, of course, familiar nonscientific examples as well. For example, if a person uses the word 'bachelor' so that it applies to unmarried women, then, though the person may win social esteem in some circles, the word is not being used correctly in English. Thus, the distinction between correct and incorrect usage is a central feature of our conception of a communal language. What determines what is correct and incorrect is *social consensus*.

The sort of consensus that determines whether usage is correct or incorrect is not contractual or reached by any sort of explicit agreement. Speakers are given different weights. People delegate decision making authority in some domains to experts with special qualifications, whether those of a scientist or tribal shaman. Individuals in a speech community give varying degrees of positive respect to members of a community, and the weight represents the degree to which one would trust the other as an authority about some aspect of the language, for example, about the meaning of a word. Such weights may be applied in our aggregation procedure to find a consensual weight. It is immediately obvious, however, that some complication is necessary, because the weight that a person assigns to another will depend on the specific sort of linguistic question, the specific semantic relation, for example, under consideration. A person who is expert in one area is not expert in another, and it is appropriate that he should receive different weights for his answers to questions about semantic relations in the two domains. Thus, the weighting should be conceived of as relative to a specific semantic question.

The application of our method of language is, of course, completely idealized. The advantage is that it amalgamates the total information members have about each other as linguistic authorities. Great weight may be given to some member of the community indirectly through a *chain* of respect. This articulates the fact that some members of the community, for example, a scientific authority in some domain, may indirectly acquire great weight in the process described, that is, their semantic probability assignment may strongly determine the consensual assignment, even though very few members of the group know anything about them. As a simple example of a short chain, some person may assign high positive respect to their own doctor as a linguistic authority in the domain of biological words, and this doctor may, in turn, assign a very high weight to some research biologist, who is unknown to his patient, with the result that the research biologist strongly influences the consensual semantics in the biological domain.

Since the consensual model aggregates the total information in the community, we can say that the consensual semantic probability relations provide us with the *correct* semantic relations for the communal language. It is clear, of course, that for the purpose of writing a dictionary, or other qualitative lexicons, the quantities are ignored. Nevertheless, such relations provide us with a more exact set of semantic relations. The relations of unity and zero, corresponding to simple semantic implication and contradiction, are but a special, and to some extent, unusual case. Most semantic relations are grey.

17. CONSENSUS AS FICTION

It is to be immediately noted that both the single speaker and the community do not have time for even rudimentary calculations of sort we have indicated. These calculations, though mathematically simple, require a rational regimentation of information that is uncommon. According to utility theory, the cost of calculation must be figured in any rational decision, and, except for a few mathematical wizards, people find such calculations onerous. Hence, rather than finding an expectation or consensus, rather than constructing them, they are simple posited, simply postulated. No one does amalgamate the information within a language to determine consensus. Rather, on the contrary, we indulge in a fiction. We do, no doubt, have some simple and rather vague rules to guide our behavior, for example, to say the simplest relevant thing, as Grice [1975] suggests. We have some equally simple rules for determining the meaning of words in the language, for example, to ask the most respected speakers with the relevant expertise. We know, however, that 'relevant' is a fudge word. When we think of a communal language, we posit a fiction, an ideal consensus, and we attach some simple rules for approximating or ascertaining what the consensus would be. That consensus constitutes that communal language, the conversion of idiolects into a language.

Fortunately, when we reflect on the proposed model, we are warrented in concluding that information contained in the group would, in fact, yield a consensus as a point of convergence if the calculations were actually made. Thus, we may conclude that the language, though a fiction in fact, could, in principle, be discovered. It is clear enough, given this situation, why an individual linguist should allow himself to use only one informant, himself, when constructing a linguistic theory. When one employs no method of aggregation, then the data from multiple speakers appears only to confuse and confound the problem. Our proposal is that there is, in fact, an acceptable method for amalgamating such information, and, therefore, that there is no need to confine the confirmation and testing of semantic theory to the information contained in a single individual.

18. CAUSATION AND CONSENSUS

We conclude this section by indicating a certain conflict between the methodology suggested here and now rather popular alternative methodology of Kirpke [1971] and Putnam [1975]. According to the latter methodology, the semantics and reference of certain expressions, certain names or predicates, are causally determined by certain initial acts of reference. To take an example from Putnam, there are certain initial acts of reference that pick out a substance, say water, and the meaning of the term 'water' is derived from these initial referential actions. It is interesting to notice that this thesis combines rather poorly with a second thesis which is that we might subsequently discover the true nature of the substance in question, in this case, that the substance is H_2O. For, it is almost certain that the substance initially referred to a water will, in fact, not be H_2O but some much more complicated mixture containing only a large measure of H_2O. According to the consensual model, the semantics of the word in question, for example, 'water', will be influenced by both the initial referential acts, because these will, in turn, influence ordinary employment of the term 'water', and by scientific knowledge, which will influence the scientific use of the expression. The consensual semantic probability relation between the statement that something is water and the statement that it is H_2O will be influenced by both the ordinary and the technical use of the expression 'water' and by the extent to which the vulgar are inclined to delegate linguistic authority to the experts in this domain. My projection of the admittedly fictional consensual semantic probability is that it is high, over .5, but surely less than unity. It should be noted here that such a probability assignment has nothing whatever to do with our expectation concerning the frequency of samples of pure water in the actual world. This is a probability relation that holds for all possible worlds and is, therefore, a purely semantic relationship. It seems clear to me, moreover, that this semantic relation is a weaker relation than the relation between the statement that someone is a bachelor and the statement that the person is unmarried. The latter example is as good an example as any of a semantic probability equal to unity. That is why it is so often used. The example concerning the word 'water' is both more interesting and more controversial, and that means simply that the consensual semantic probability is lower.

The advantage of the present approach over the rather popular referential approach to semantics is that the present theory allows us to incorporate information about acts of reference as well as information about scientific discovery into our semantics without thereby supposing that such initial acts of reference or subsequent scientific knowledge have a monopoly in semantics. Acts of reference and other knowledge are *factors*, perhaps vectors of influence, that determine the semantic probability relations of individuals as well as the weight they give to others as linguistic authorities. We may obtain the result, through the proposed method, that a word is commonly applied to something but does not really apply to it; for example, we might say that the stuff commonly called 'water' is not really water but an impure mixture of water and other substances. In this case, the weight of scientific experts overwhelms the original acts of reference, but this need not always be the case. The truth of the matter can be formulated very simply. There is a plurality of factors that are relevant to determining the semantics of a communal language. Philosophers are want to construct theories that select one of these factors as *the* determinant of semantics. But this is a mistake, the sort of mistake that leads to interesting and valuable theoretical construction, but a mistake nonetheless. Communal language is determined by a consensus that amalgamates the total relevant information in a language community in a coherent manner.

An individual may summarize the semantic information he possesses in his idiolect in the form of semantic probability relations. At this level, we have a variety of diverse probability relations that represent a summary of referential and ratiocinative linguistic behavior and reflection. This is a coherent summary of complex and diffuse information. To obtain the communal language, individual summaries must again be combined, amalgamated and aggregated to obtain a coherent conception. This amalgamation, we have suggested, is a fiction, though one that, in principle, could be calculated. To do so, we would need to require that individuals represent their complex and diffuse information about the linguistic authority of others as an appropriate weight which reflects how much authority they are willing to delegate to other members of the community. We may then combine these individual semantic probabilities and weights in a mathematically simple manner. Given rather plausible conditions, we would obtain the consensual semantic relations as the point of convergence within the community. This consensus is the coherent amalgamation of linguistic information in a speech community. It is, mathematically speaking, a simple aggregation. It is not that language just happens to be consensual, on the contrary, it is consensus that defines a language.

PART TWO

THE FORMAL FOUNDATIONS OF RATIONAL
CONSENSUS

CHAPTER SIX

ALLOCATION AND ORDERING BY WEIGHTED
ARITHMETIC AVERAGING – AN AXIOMATIC APPROACH

1. INTRODUCTION

As a result of the efforts of a generation of decision theorists, it is now widely accepted that axiomatic theory is a valuable analytical tool for evaluating proposed decision methods. The program of axiomatizing decision criteria, initiated by Arrow [1951], has produced a sophisticated and extensive literature. This program has been at once modest and ambitious, modest in its recognition that rational choice is context sensitive and in its willingness to countenance impossibility theorems, ambitious in its attempt to provide axiomatic foundations for the many varieties of group decision problems.

In this chapter we present axiomatic characterizations of several decision methods based on weighted arithmetic averaging. Each of the cases which we consider involves the problem of aggregating a multiplicity of perspectives or opinions. The perspectives in question may be those of a single individual approaching a problem from different points of view, or of a group of individuals. In the former case we speak of aggregation yielding an *integration* of the individual's perspectives, in the latter a *consensus* of group opinion. In what follows we shall employ the language of group decisionmaking and consensus, while keeping in mind that the formal models we investigate admit a wider interpretation.

In every case which we consider there will be a group of at least two individuals, and one or more numerical decision variables. We assume a labeling $1, \ldots, n$ of the individuals and a labeling $x_1, \ldots, x_k$ of the decision variables. Individual opinions are registered in an $n \times k$ matrix $A = (a_{ij})$, where a_{ij} is the value assigned by individual i to variable x_j. The matrix A may be regarded as an input of the decision process. The cases which we study are distinguished by the desired output. In Sections 2–5 we consider the problem of mapping A to a *vector* $(a_1, \ldots, a_k)$, where a_j represents the consensual value of x_j. Our results in these sections are new and have important applications to allocation problems, including the problem of consensual probability. These results also provide a foundation for the iterated weighting scheme discussed in Chapters Two and Three. In Section 6 we view the variables as a set of alternatives and the numbers a_{ij} as "scores" assigned to these alternatives, and consider the classical problem of mapping A to an *ordering* of alternatives. Although the axiomatics of this sort of aggregation has been extensively treated by social choice theorists, we include a sketch of several known results of particular interest, with additional references to the literature.

2. ALLOCATION PROBLEMS

Suppose that a group of n individuals is seeking consensual numerical values of a sequence of k decision variables, $x_1, \ldots, x_k$. We shall call such a decision problem an *allocation problem* if the values of these variables are constrained by the requirements (1) $x_j \geqslant 0, j = 1, \ldots, k$ and (2) $x_1 + \ldots + x_k = s$, for some fixed $s > 0$. Examples of allocation problems abound, and include such familiar problems as (1) assigning probabilities to a sequence of k pairwise exclusive, exhaustive propositions ($s = 1$) and (2) allocating a fixed sum of money or other resource, s, among k projects. Note that a problem involving the apparently more general constraint $x_1 + \ldots + x_k \leqslant s$ may be reformulated as an allocation problem $x_1 + \ldots + x_k + y = s$, where y is the optimization theorist's familiar "slack variable."

Suppose that individual opinions as to the most appropriate values of these variables are registered in the $n \times k$ matrix $A = (a_{ij})$, where a_{ij} is the value assigned by individual i to variable x_j. We assume that the constraints defining an allocation problem apply both to the individual opinions reported in A and to the final set of consensual values. Furthermore we require that a method for aggregating group opinion be applicable to every possible configuration of opinions. Let $\mathscr{A}(n, k; s)$ denote the set of all $n \times k$ matrices A with nonnegative entries and all row sums equal to s, and let $\mathscr{A}(k; s)$ denote the set of all vectors $a = (a_1, \ldots, a_k)$ with nonnegative entries and $a_1 + \ldots + a_k = s$. Allowing for the widest possible initial range of aggregation methods, we make the following definition:

DEFINITION. *An allocation aggregation method* (AAM) *is a function F*: $\mathscr{A}(n, k; s) \rightarrow \mathscr{A}(k; s)$, *for fixed positive integers n and k and fixed s > 0.*

The familiar arithmetic mean yields an AAM by the rule: $F(A) = (a_1, \ldots, a_k)$, where a_j is the arithmetic mean, $(a_{1j} + \ldots + a_{nj})/n$, of the entries in the j-th column of A. This method gives, in some sense, equal weight to the opinions of all individuals in the decisionmaking group. More generally, any set of weights $w_1, \ldots, w_n$, nonnegative and summing to 1, yields an AAM by the rule: $F(A) = (a_1, \ldots, a_k)$, where a_j is the weighted arithmetic mean, $w_1 a_{1j} + \ldots + w_n a_{nj}$, of the entries in the j-th column of A. When individuals differ in expertise, a weighted arithmetic mean with unequal weights may be an appropriate way to reflect such differences. In the next section we present, among other results, a characterization of the set of AAMs based on weighted arithmetic averaging, thus providing criteria for employing such aggregation methods. Proofs of the theorems stated in the next two sections appear in a technical appendix at the end of the chapter. See also Wagner [1981 b].

3. AAMS BASED ON WEIGHTED ARITHMETIC MEANS

Consider an AAM F constructed as above from a sequence of weights w_1, $\ldots, w_n$. For each matrix $A \in \mathscr{A}(n, k; s)$ let A_j denote the j-th column of A, and let $F(A) = (a_1, \ldots, a_k)$. It is easy to check that F has the following properties:

1. IA (*Irrelevance of Alternatives*): For all $A, B \in \mathscr{A}(n, k: s)$ $A_j = B_j \Rightarrow a_j = b_j$.

2. Z (*Zero Unanimity*): For all $A \in \mathscr{A}(n, k; s)$, if A_j consists entirely of zeros, then $a_j = 0$.

3. LN (*Label Neutrality*): If σ is a permutation on the set $\{1, \ldots, k\}$, for all $A, B \in \mathscr{A}(n, k; s)$, if $B_j = A_{\sigma(j)}$ for $j = 1, \ldots, k$, then $b_j = a_{\sigma(j)}$.

4. SLN (*Strong Label Neutrality*): For all $A, B \in \mathscr{A}(n, k; s)$ $A_{j_1} = B_{j_2} \Rightarrow a_{j_1} = b_{j_2}$.

Property Z states a very weak unanimity condition: if all individuals assign x_j the value zero, F does the same. Properties IA, LN, and SLN are invariance conditions of varying strength. IA specifies that if values assigned by individuals to x_j are unchanged, changes in the values assigned by these individuals to variables other than x_j do not change the final value assigned to x_j by F. LN specifics that a variable be given no special consideration by F in virtue of its particular label — a relabeling of variables results, under F, in the same relabeling of the final values assigned to those variables. As noted below, SLN is equivalent to the conjunction of LN and IA.

THEOREM 6.1. *An AAM satisfies* SLN *if and only if it satisfies* IA *and* LN.

Note that when $k = 2$, IA holds trivially. When $k \geqslant 3$, however, IA is a property of some consequence. Indeed, when supplemented by the weak property Z, it implies SLN.

THEOREM 6.2. *If $k \geqslant 3$, an AAM F: $\mathscr{A}(n, k; s) \to \mathscr{A}(k; s)$ satisfies SLN if it satisfies IA and Z.*

It is of interest at this point to note an important consequence of the property SLN. If F satisfies SLN, then the value assigned by F to each variable x_j is a function exclusively of the values assigned by individuals to x_j, and independent of j. More formally, let $[0, s]$ denote the closed interval of real numbers between 0 and s, and let $[0, s]^n = \{(t_1, \ldots, t_n): t_i \in [0, s]\}$. (Note that the columns of a matrix $A \in \mathscr{A}(n, k; s)$ correspond in a natural way to members of $[0, s]^n$.)

THEOREM 6.3. *Let F: $\mathscr{A}(n, k; s) \to \mathscr{A}(k; s)$ satisfy SLN. Then there exists a function H: $[0, s]^n \to [0, s]$ such that for all $A = (a_{ij}) \in \mathscr{A}(n, k; s)$, $F(A) = (a_1, \ldots, a_k)$, where $a_j = H(a_{1j}, \ldots, a_{nj})$.*

We may now characterize, for the case $k \geqslant 3$, those AAMs based on weighted arithmetic averaging.

THEOREM 6.4. *If $k \geqslant 3$, an AAM F: $\mathscr{A}(n, k; s) \to \mathscr{A}(k; s)$ satisfies IA and Z if and only if there exists a sequence of weights $w_1, \ldots, w_n$, nonnegative and summing to one, such that for all $A = (a_{ij}) \in \mathscr{A}(n, k; s)$, $F(A) = (a_1, \ldots, a_k)$, where $a_j = w_1 a_{1j} + \ldots + w_n a_{nj}, j = 1, \ldots k$.*

We emphasize that the foregoing theorem holds only when there are at least three decision variables ($k \geqslant 3$). When $k = 2$, since IA holds trivially, it is easy to see that the conjunction of IA and Z need not imply SLN. The most we seem to be able to accomplish in this case is a characterization of AAMs satisfying SLN and Z. As noted below, such restrictions admit a wide variety of nonlinear amalgamation methods.

THEOREM 6.5. *An AAM F: $\mathscr{A}(n, 2; s) \to \mathscr{A}(2; s)$ satisfies SLN and Z if and only if there is a function h: $[-s/2, s/2]^n \to [-s/2, s/2]$, where*

(1)   *h is odd ($h(-\alpha_1, \ldots, -\alpha_n) = -h(\alpha_1, \ldots, \alpha_n)$),*

and

(2)   *$h(s/2, \ldots, s/2) = s/2$,*

such that for all $A = (a_{ij}) \in \mathscr{A}(n, 2; s)$, $F(A) = (a_1, a_2)$, where $a_j = h(a_{1j} - s/2, \ldots, a_{nj} - s/2) + s/2, j = 1, 2$.

In particular h (and, hence, H) may be any weighted arithmetic mean. However, nonlinear functions such as $h(\alpha_1, \ldots, \alpha_n) = [(\alpha_1^3 + \ldots \alpha_n^3)/n]^{1/3}$ also serve here to define AAMs satisfying SLN and Z.[1] When $k = 2$, short of actually positing linearity, there seems to be no obvious way to isolate the AAMs based on arithmetic averaging.

Let us summarize our results thus far. In the case of an allocation problem involving at least three variables, Theorem 6.4 tells us that an AAM satisfying Z and IA (equivalently, Z and SLN) must be based on weighted arithmetic averaging. When there are only two variables, however, Z and SLN allow an AAM to be based on a class of odd multivariable functions which properly includes the class of weighted arithmetic means (Theorem 6.5). These results offer substantial guidance in the choice of an AAM, given a prior decision to employ an amalgamation method satisfying Z and IA (respectively, Z and SLN). How reasonable is it to require that amalgamation satisfy these properties?

Consider first property Z, which, as noted earlier, is a very weak unanimity condition. Unless one has reason to believe that the decisionmakers are systematically biased in their evaluation of one or more variables, it is surely reasonable to respect their unanimity in assigning a variable the value zero. Moreover, if the output of an AAM is regarded simply as a summary of group opinion, unanimity will of necessity be respected. As for IA, it is easy to prove the following analogue of Theorem 6.3:

THEOREM 6.6. *Let* F: $\mathscr{A}(n, k; s) \to \mathscr{A}(k; s)$ *satisfy IA. Then for* $j = 1, \ldots, k$, *there exist functions* H_j: $[0, s]^n \to [0, s]$ *such that for all* $A = (a_{ij}) \in \mathscr{A}(n, k; s)$, $F(A) = (a_1, \ldots, a_k)$, *where* $a_j = H_j (a_{1j}, \ldots, a_{nj})$.

Thus if F satisfies IA, the value assigned by F to each variable x_j is a function (possibly dependent on j) exclusively of the values assigned by individuals to x_j. Given the values assigned by individuals to x_j, values assigned by individuals to alternative variables are, in short, irrelevant. Indeed, if $k \geqslant 3$ and IA is supplemented by Z, the above functions H_j are identical (Theorems 6.2 and 6.3) and equal to some weighted arithmetic mean (Theorem 6.4).

Despite its somewhat formidable name,[2] IA is a rather weak condition. It postulates the irrelevance of the values of certain variables in a context where there are built-in constraints on certain sums of these variables. Because of these allocation constraints, issues have, in a sense, already been sorted out among variables evaluated in a matrix A. The value assigned by an individual to x_j is a function of s and the values he assigns to variables other than x_j.

Thus, in assigning a final value to x_j an AAM satisfying IA "ignores" the values assigned by individuals to variables other than x_j in a limited sense.

Indeed, we would argue that the burden of justification lies with those who propose not to adopt IA in choosing an AAM. It is easy, of course, to construct AAMs for which IA fails. For example, the "benefit-of-the-doubt AAM," which identifies the maximum values assigned by individuals to each variable and normalizes these so that the resulting sum is s, clearly violates IA.[3] This method can be attacked for giving too much weight to the opinion of a single individual, just as it can be defended for its (unidirectional) sensitivity to the perceptions of a single individual.

But such exchanges are not a fruitful way of evaluating a method of amalgamating opinion. No informed choice of an AAM can be made in the absence of an axiomatic characterization of that AAM, or of some natural class of methods of which it is a member.

4. THE CONSENSUS OF PROBABILITIES

As noted in Section 2, the assignment of probabilities to a sequence of pairwise exclusive, exhaustive propositions is an allocation problem with $s = 1$. Specializations of the theorems of Section 3 thus yield interesting results on the amalgamation of probability distributions of a set of individuals. In particular, *if there are at least three propositions, and if an* AAM *assigns a probability to each proposition purely as a function of the probabilities assigned to that proposition by individuals, and respects their agreement in assigning a proposition the probability zero, then the* AAM *is based on weighted arithmetic averaging.*[4]

In this section we present a probability amalgamation theorem which removes the finiteness restriction on the set of alternatives. We thus switch to a measure-theoretic point of view and consider the amalgamation of a sequence of probability measures on a fixed, possibly infinite, σ-algebra of events.

Let X be a nonempty set and $\mathscr{S}$ a σ-algebra on X. Let $\mathscr{P}(\mathscr{S})$ denote the set of probability measures on $\mathscr{S}$ and let $\mathscr{P}(\mathscr{S})^n = \{(p_1, \ldots, p_n): p_i \in \mathscr{P}(\mathscr{S}), i = 1, \ldots, n\}$. A *probability amalgamation method* (PAM) is a function $F: \mathscr{P}(\mathscr{S})^n \to \mathscr{P}(\mathscr{S})$. Clearly each sequence of weights, $w_1, \ldots, w_n$, nonnegative and summing to one, gives rise to a PAM by the rule: $F(p_1, \ldots, p_n) = p$, where, for all $A \in \mathscr{S}, p(A) = w_1 p_1(A) + \ldots + w_n p_n(A)$. Such PAMs have the property of determining the measure of each event purely as a function of the individual measures ascribed to that event, and independently of the label of that event. Indeed, with a single exception, if a PAM satisfies this property, then it must be based on weighted arithmetic averaging. In view of Theorem 6.5 we would of course not expect such a result to hold for "small" σ-algebras such as $\mathscr{S}_A = \{\phi, A, X-A, X\}$, where A is a proper non-empty subset of X. Let us call a nontrivial σ-algebra on X *tertiary* if it is not equal to any $\mathscr{S}_A$. It is easy to see that $\mathscr{S}$ is tertiary if and only if it contains at least three nonempty pairwise disjoint events. A modification of the proof of Theorem 6.4 yields a proof of the following theorem:

THEOREM 6.7. *Let $\mathscr{S}$ be a tertiary σ-algebra on X and let $F: \mathscr{P}(\mathscr{S})^n \to \mathscr{P}(\mathscr{S})$ be a PAM for which there exists a function $H: [0, 1]^n \to [0, 1]$ such that $F(p_1, \ldots, p_n) = p$, where for all $A \in \mathscr{S}, p(A) = H(p_1(A), \ldots, p_n(A))$. Then H is a weighted arithmetic mean.*[5]

We remark in conclusion that for the trivial σ-algebra $\mathscr{S} = \{\phi, X\}$ every PAM is based on weighted arithmetic averaging, since $\mathscr{S}$ admits only one probability measure. As for the σ-algebras $\mathscr{S}_A = \{\phi, A, X-A, X\}$, it is easy to prove a result complementary to that of Theorem 6.7, where the function H must belong to the class described in Theorem 6.5.

5. FOUNDATIONS FOR ITERATED WEIGHTING SCHEMES

Theorem 6.4 may also be used to identify a set of decisionmaking conditions from which we may derive the iterated weighting schemes discussed in Chapters 2, 3, and 7. For simplicity of exposition we treat only the case in which a single group of individuals constructs all of the relevant weight matrices. It will be clear how to modify our discussion to encompass the more general case in which possibly different groups construct weight matrices at different levels.

Suppose that n individuals are responsible for assigning values to k decision variables. We claim that under the following four conditions, iterated weighting is the indicated decision method:

I. The original decision problem is an allocation problem involving at least three variables ($k \geqslant 3$).

II. There are at least three individuals ($n \geqslant 3$).

III. Failing consensus, the values assigned by these decisionmakers to the initial variables are to be amalgamated by a method satisfying Z and IA.

IV.   These same decisionmakers are responsible for determining the values of any auxiliary decision variables required as a consequence of satisfying condition III, and, failing consensus, their opinions regarding the most appropriate values of such auxiliary variables are to be amalgamated by a method satisfying Z and IA.

The derivation of iterated weighting from these four principles is straightforward. By I, III, and Theorem 6.4, opinions registered in A, failing consensus, must be amalgamated by weighted averaging with weights nonnegative and summing to one. Determination of these weights is therefore an allocation problem which, by II, involves at least three first order auxiliary weight variables. By IV, the evaluation of these variables is to be carried out, failing consensus, by amalgamating individual opinions on the matter by a method satisfying Z and IA. Hence, by Theorem 6.4, the group must seek a set of consensual second order weights, nonnegative and summing to one, with which to average opinions regarding the first order weights. Determination of these weights poses a further allocation problem involving at least three second order auxiliary decision variables. Thus by IV and Theorem 6.4, failing consensus on this issue, the group must seek consensual third order weights with which to average their opinions regarding values of the second order weights. Each time consensus fails the above conditions dictate the introduction of higher order auxiliary variables. Condition IV is essentially a "looping" instruction. As stated, it specifies no limit on the number of higher order weight matrices constructed by the group, but as a practical matter, it might be supplemented by an instruction to stop the process when an acceptable approximation of consensus emerges, or when no such approximation has emerged at some predetermined level.

6. CONSENSUAL ORDERINGS

By an *ordering* of a set S we mean a binary relation R which is complete ($\forall x, y \in S, xRy$ or yRx) and transitive ($\forall x, y, z \in S, xRy \& yRz \Rightarrow xRz$). Associated to each ordering R is its "asymmetric part" P, defined by $xPy \Leftrightarrow xRy \in \sim yRx$, and its "symmetric part" I, defined by $xIy \Leftrightarrow xRy$ and yRx. When, as is frequently the case in applications, S is a set of policy alternatives ordered by the preferences of an individual or a group, xPy is interpreted as asserting that alternative x is strictly preferred to alternative y, xIy as asserting indifference between x and y, and xRy weak preference (i.e., strict preference or indifference) for x over y. The relations R and P contain equivalent information, since $xRy \Leftrightarrow xPy$ or ($\sim xPy$ and $\sim yPx$).

In this section we consider the problem of finding a consensual ordering of a set of alternatives. We suppose that n individuals, labeled $1, \ldots, n$ and k alternatives, labeled $1, \ldots, k$ are involved. *Throughout this section it will always be assumed that $n \geqslant 2$ and $k \geqslant 3$.* Our main concern in this section will be to analyze methods of producing a consensual ordering from an $n \times k$ matrix $A = (a_{ij})$, where a_{ij} is a numerical score assigned by individual i to alternative j. Before treating this type of decision problem, however, we offer a brief sketch of the Arrow Impossibility Theorem, since this famous limitative theorem of social welfare theory has continued to be an important point of reference for subsequent work on consensual ordering.

The classical problem of social welfare theory is to investigate methods for producing from every possible "profile" of individual preferential orderings $(R_1, \ldots, R_n)$ a consensual, or "societal" ordering R. Here R_i denotes the preferential ordering of individual i, and, as usual, P_i and P denote the respective strict orders associated to R_i and R. Any mapping from the set of all preference profiles to the set of orderings is called a *social welfare function*. The aim of social welfare theory is to sort through the set of social welfare functions and identify those functions which are in some sense rational and democratic. The tool employed in this enterprise is axiomatic theory. One isolates the desirable properties of an acceptable social welfare function, posits these properties as axioms, and then seeks models of this axiom system, i.e., social welfare functions which satisfy all of the axioms. In one version of Arrow's analysis, the following apparently unobjectionable properties are stipulated:

1. WP (*Weak Pareto Property*): For any alternatives x and y, if everyone strictly prefers x to y $(xP_iy, i = 1, \ldots, n)$, then xPy.

2. IIA (*Independence of Irrelevant Alternatives*): For any profiles $(R_1, \ldots, R_n)$ and $(R_1', \ldots, R_n')$ and any alternatives x and y, if for each $i = 1, \ldots, n$, R_i and R_i' rank x and y in exactly the same way $(xR_iy \Leftrightarrow xR_i'y$ and $yR_ix \Leftrightarrow yR_i'x)$, then R and R' rank x and y in exactly the same way.

The social welfare functions satisfying the above two axioms are, however, not particularly attractive.

THEOREM 6.8. (Arrow [1951]). *Any social welfare function satisfying* WP *and* IIA *is dictatorial, i.e., there is an individual i whose strict preferences are always incorporated in the social ordering (for all profiles and all alternatives $x, y, xP_iy \Rightarrow xPy$).*

Attempts at what A. K. Sen [1977] has labeled "Arrow-dodging" have ranged

from taking issue with the desirability of condition IIA to relaxing the requirement that a social welfare function be applicable to all profiles, or even that
it produce an ordering. Readers interested in the details will find an excellent
summary in Sen's article. Our interest here is in describing a different kind
of response to Arrow's theorem. According to the point of view which we
wish to investigate, Arrow's result is seen, at least in retrospect, as a not-too-
surprising outcome of limiting the input of individuals to a simple report of
their preferences. Suppose, for example, that individuals were allowed to
assign numerical scores to the alternatives in question. Perhaps this extended
informational base, which offers the possibility of recording and comparing
intensities of preference, is the proper starting point for a theory of social
choice.

In the remainder of this section we shall thus suppose that the information
from which an ordering is to be derived consists of an $n \times k$ matrix $A = (a_{ij})$,
where a_{ij} is a numerical score assigned by individual i to alternative j. We assume as the minimal information conveyed by A that $a_{ix} > a_{iy}$ means that
individual i strictly prefers alternative x to alternative y.

As in earlier sections we wish to investigate methods of amalgamation
applicable to every possible array of scores. Let $\mathscr{A}_{nxk}$ denote the set of all
$n \times k$ matrices with real entries, and let $\mathscr{R}_k$ denote the set of all orderings of
the set of alternatives $\{1, \ldots, k\}$. We formalize the notion of an amalgamation method in this context as follows:

DEFINITION. A *social welfare functional* (SWFL) *is a function* $F : \mathscr{A}_{nxk} \rightarrow \mathscr{R}_k$.

Given a SWFL F and $A \in \mathscr{A}_{nxk}$, we shall denote the ordering $F(A)$ by R_A
and the asymmetric part of R_A by P_A. Suppose that we have a sequence of
weights $w_1, \ldots, w_n$, *positive* and summing to one. Given a matrix A we may
use these weights to determine consensual scores for each of the alternatives
and order the alternatives by the magnitude of their consensual scores. More
formally, we define a SWFL F by the condition

$$xR_A y \Leftrightarrow \sum_{i=1}^{n} w_i a_{ix} \geqslant \sum_{i=1}^{n} w_i a_{iy},$$

for any alternatives x and y. It is easy to check that F has the following
properties:

P (*Strong Pareto Condition*): Given alternatives x and y, if for all i, $a_{ix} \geqslant a_{iy}$, then $xR_A y$; if, for all i, $a_{ix} \geqslant a_{iy}$ and there is some individual j such that
$a_{jx} > a_{jy}$, then $xP_A y$.

I (*Independence of Irrelevant Alternatives*): Given A, $A' \in \mathscr{A}_{n \times k}$, if columns x and y of A are identical with their counterparts in A', then $x R_A y \Leftrightarrow x R_A' y$.

T (*Translation Invariance*): If for $A = (a_{ij})$ and $A' = (a'_{ij}) \in \mathscr{A}_{n \times k}$, there is a sequence of constants $b_1, \ldots, b_n$ such that for $i = 1, \ldots, n$ and $j = 1, \ldots, k$, $a'_{ij} = a_{ij} + b_i$, then $R_A = R_A'$.

While the above three conditions do not precisely characterize the class of SWFLs described above, they do imply for any SWFL satisfying them that arithmetic aggregation plays a major, if not completely determinative, role in the specification of that SWFL:

THEOREM 6.9. *If* $F: \mathscr{A}_{n \times k} \to \mathscr{R}_k$ *satisfies P, I, and T, then there is a sequence of weights* $w_1, \ldots, w_n$, *nonnegative and summing to one, such that for all* $A \in \mathscr{A}_{n \times k}$ *and all alternatives x and y,*

$$\sum_{i=1}^{n} w_i a_{ix} > \sum_{i=1}^{n} w_i a_{iy} \Rightarrow x P_A y.$$

Proofs of this theorem appear in Blackwell and Girshick [1954] and Gevers [1979].[6] Note that one or more weights may take the value zero, and that the inequality between weighted averages is sufficient, but not necessary for the relation P_A to hold. How reasonable is it to require that a SWFL satisfy P, I, and T? Condition P specifies that if all individuals score alternative x at least as highly as alternative y, then the consensual ordering ranks x at or above the level of y; and if, in addition, at least one individual assigns x a greater score than y, the consensual ordering ranks x strictly above y. Such a condition appears uncontroversial.

Condition I requires that the consensual ordering of any two alternatives depend only on the scores assigned by individuals to these alternatives — scores assigned to other alternatives are irrelevant. Condition I is considerably weaker than the classical Arrow condition IIA. IIA, by requiring that the consensual ordering of any two alternatives be derived from the restrictions of individual orderings to that pair of alternatives, rules out any considerations of depth of preference, as indicated, say, by the number of alternatives ranked between these two. When individuals assign numerical scores to two alternatives, however, there is ostensibly depth of preference information incorporated in these scores, for example in the differences or ratios between scores. Condition I does not rule out the use of such information.

Indeed, the invariance condition T may be seen as strengthening I by rendering irrelevant certain comparisons between scores. In particular, interpersonal comparisons between score *levels* are rendered meaningless by T since inequalities between scores assigned to an alternative by two individuals are not preserved under individual translation. On the other hand, the *differences* between scores assigned by an individual to two alternatives are invariant under translations and thus comparable between individuals. Indeed, Theorem 6.9 shows exactly how a SWFL satisfying P, I, and T takes account of such differences. For the rule

$$\sum_{i=1}^{n} w_i a_{ix} > \sum_{i=1}^{n} w_i a_{iy} \Rightarrow x P_A y$$

may be written equivalently as

$$\sum_{i=1}^{n} w_i (a_{ix} - a_{iy}) > 0 \Rightarrow x P_A y.$$

The question, then, is whether T is an appropriate invariance condition. Clearly the strength of the relevant invariance condition should vary inversely with the "rigidity" of the scoring mechanism. If scores are meaningful just up to individual translation, i.e., if individuals are scoring alternatives on what measurement theorists[7] call "interval scales with the same unit and possibly different zero points," then T is a reasonable invariance condition. If the scales of measurement on which scores are reported are less rigid than this, or rigid in a different way, then T is not appropriate and weighted arithmetic averaging lacks compelling axiomatic justification as a method of amalgamation.

The foregoing point is best illustrated by several examples. As an example of scores rigid in way different from those considered above, we may take the case of scores reported on what measurement theorists call "individual ratio scales." Here the relevant domain of a SWFL is $\mathscr{A}_{n \times k}^{+}$, the set of $n \times k$ matrices with exclusively positive entries, and the relevant invariance condition is

M (Multiplication Invariance): If for $A = (a_{ij})$ and $A' = (a'_{ij}) \in \mathscr{A}_{n \times k}^{+}$, there is a sequence of positive constants $c_1, \ldots, c_n$ such that for all i and j, $a'_{ij} = c_i a_{ij}$, then $R_A = R_{A'}$.

In conjunction with P and I (restricted to $\mathscr{A}_{n \times k}^{+}$), M implies the use of weighted *geometric* means to produce a consensual ordering of alternatives:

THEOREM 6.10. *If $F: \mathscr{A}_{n \times k}^{+} \to \mathscr{R}_k$ satisfies P, I, and M, then there is a sequence of weights, $w_1, \ldots, w_n$, nonnegative and summing to one, such that for all $A = (a_{ij}) \in \mathscr{A}_{n \times k}^{+}$ and all alternatives x and y,*

$$\prod_{i=1}^{n} a_{ix}^{w_i} > \prod_{i=1}^{n} a_{iy}^{w_i} \Rightarrow xP_A y.$$

Condition M correlates with the assumption of interpersonal comparability of score ratios, and Theorem 6.10 shows exactly how a SWFL takes account of such ratios. For one may formulate the condition guaranteeing strict consensual preference equivalently as: $\prod_{i=1}^{n} (a_{ix}/a_{iy})^{w_i} > 1 \Rightarrow xP_A y$. Theorem 6.10 follows immediately from Theorem 6.9 by taking logarithms. While geometric means may seem to be rather exotic amalgamation functions they have in fact been employed in practical decisionmaking.[8] The point of introducing them here is to illustrate that arithmetic aggregation occupies no *a priori* privileged position in constructing SWFLs. On the other hand, Theorem 6.10 reveals a further class of decision problems which require the determination of a set of weights, thus broadening the applicability of the weighting method described in Chapters Two and Three.

As a further and particularly significant example, suppose that the most we are justified in assuming is that individuals are reporting scores on interval scales with possibly different units *and* possibly different zero points. The appropriate invariance condition with which to supplement P and I is then

CN (*Cardinal Noncomparability*): If for $A = (a_{ij})$ and $A' = (a_{ij}')$, there is a sequence of real constants $b_1, \ldots, b_n$ and a sequence of positive real constants $c_1, \ldots, c_n$ such that for all i and j, $a_{ij}' = c_i a_{ij} + b_i$, then $R_A = R_{A'}$.

Since scores in the above context are meaningful only up to positive affine transformations $a_{ij} \to c_i a_{ij} + b_i$, it is not meaningful to compare score levels or score differences across individuals. This lack of rigidity so impoverishes the informational base provided by a matrix A that we find ourselves confronting another version of Arrow's Theorem:

THEOREM 6.11. *Any SWFL satisfying P, I, and CN is dictatorial*, i.e., *there is an individual i such that for all $A \in \mathscr{A}_{n \times k}$ and all alternatives x and y*, if $a_{ix} > a_{iy}$, *then $xP_A y$.*

The above theorem follows immediately from results of d'Aspremont and Gevers [1977, Theorem 2] and Gevers [1979, Theorem 2].[9] This theorem has important consequences for the classical social welfare problem in which the score a_{ij} denotes the personal utility to individual i resulting from the adoption of alternative j as a social policy. For while such utilities, generated by the method of von Neumann-Morgenstern bets,[10] are cardinal, i.e. meaningful up to positive affine transformations, we possess no empirical evidence about human beings that justifies the assumption that a unit of utility on one individual's scale is comparable to a unit or someone else's scale. Thus *CN* appears to be the relevant invariance condition when amalgamating utility scores.

Viewed from the most pessimistic perspective this suggests that cardinal utilities have nothing to offer over and above ordinal utilities, which represent preferences by their magnitudes, but are meaningful only up to transformation by arbitrary strictly increasing functions. Indeed, if one holds steadfastly to the view that neither utility levels nor utility gains or losses are to be compared cross individuals, then Theorems 6.9 and 6.11 constitute an elegant theoretical exercise culminating in despair. The dilemma is that one wishes both to respect human individuality and thus not make gratuitous assumptions that utility differences are interpersonally comparable, and yet to provide some foundation for principles of amalgamation such as those based on weighted averaging. With characteristic eloquence, Arrow [1977] has expressed this dilemma as follows:

> In a way that I cannot articulate well and am none too sure about defending, the autonomy of individuals, an element of mutual incommensurability among people seems denied by the possibility of interpersonal comparisons. No doubt it is some such feeling as this that has made me so reluctant to shift from pure ordinalism, despite my desire to seek a basis for a theory of justice.

There is, however, a more hopeful way to view Theorem 6.11. Despite its substantial limitative import, this theorem liberates us from the imperative of finding a democratic SWFL absent any assumptions about interpersonal comparability of utilities. For it demonstrates that the avoidance of a dictatorial SWFL requires some notion of comparability among individuals. Theorems 6.9 and 6.10, and other characterizations of various principles of amalgamation, expose the type of comparability assumption correlated with a given principle. It is doubtful that we shall ever possess an understanding of individuals comprehensive enough to compare their total welfare. But a modest, case-by-case analysis of more limited problems of distributive justice may yield a consensus on the comparability assumption appropriate in a given situation. As Steven Strasnick [1979], who has initiated such a program, has forcefully argued, we should be prepared to countenance different assumptions of comparability, and hence different principles of amalgamation, in different situations. From this perspective, weighted averaging, pure utilitarianism, and Rawlsian maximin rules all have a place in the library of ethical decision methods, each catalogued by an axiomatic characterization.[11]

This library is all that theoretical analysis can furnish us. We must choose from its offerings on the basis of the empathy we have come to feel by living with others in the world.

7. TECHNICAL APPENDIX

THEOREM 6.1. *An* AAM *satisfies* SLN *if and only if it satisfies* IA *and* LN.

Proof. It is clear that SLN implies IA and LN. Suppose that F satisfies IA and LN and let $A, B \in \mathscr{A}(n, k; s)$ be such that $A_{j_1} = B_{j_2}$ Denote by B' the matrix resulting from the interchange of columns j_1 and j_2 of B. Then $A_{j_1} = B'_{j_1}$, and so $a_{j_1} = b'_{j_1}$ by IA. But by LN, $b'_{j_1} = b_{j_2}$. Hence $a_{j_1} = b_{j_2}$, as required.

THEOREM 6.2. *If* $k \geqslant 3$, *an* AAM $F: \mathscr{A}(n, k; s) \to \mathscr{A}(k; s)$ *satisfies* SLN *if it satisfies* IA *and* Z.

Proof. Let $A, B \in \mathscr{A}(n, k; s)$ be such that $A_{j_1} = B_{j_2}$, and let $[\alpha_1, \ldots, \alpha_n]^T$ denote the elements in column j_1 of A (identically, in column j_2 of B). Now choose an index j_3 different from both j_1 and j_2 and define matrices A' and B' as follows: Column j_1 of A' is $[\alpha_1, \ldots, \alpha_n]^T$; column j_3 of A' is $[s-\alpha_1, \ldots, s-\alpha_n]^T$; and all other columns of A' consist entirely of zeros. Column j_2 of B' is $[\alpha_1, \ldots, \alpha_n]^T$; column j_3 of B' is $[s-\alpha_1, \ldots, s-\alpha_n]^T$; and all other columns of B' consist entirely by zeros. By Z, F assigns the value zero to all variables corresponding to zero columns. Furthermore, the values assigned by F to all variables must sum to s for every matrix. Hence $a'_{j_1} = s\text{-}a'_{j_3}$ and $b'_{j_2} = s\text{-}b'_{j_3}$. But by IA, $a'_{j_3} = b'_{j_3}$, $a_{j_1} = a'_{j_1}$, and $b_{j_2} = b'_{j_2}$. Hence $a_{j_1} = b_{j_2}$, as required.

THEOREM 6.3. *Let* $F: \mathscr{A}(n, k; s) \to \mathscr{A}(k; s)$ *satisfy* SLN. *Then there exists a function* $H: [0, s]^n \to [0, s]$ *such that for all* $A = (a_{ij}) \in \mathscr{A}(n, k; s)$, $F(A) = (a_1, \ldots, a_k)$, *where* $a_j = H(a_{1j}, \ldots, a_{nj}), j = 1, \ldots, k$.

Proof. Let $(\alpha_1, \ldots, \alpha_n) \in [0, s]^n$. Let A be a matrix whose first column is $[\alpha_1, \ldots, \alpha_n]^T$, whose second column is $[s-\alpha_1, \ldots, s-\alpha_n]^T$, and whose remaining columns, if any, consist entirely of zeros. Set $H(\alpha_1, \ldots, \alpha_n) = a_1$, the value assigned by F to x_1. It follows immediately by the invariance property SLN that H has the desired property.

THEOREM 6.4. *If* $k \geqslant 3$, *an* AAM $F: \mathscr{A}(n, k; s) \to \mathscr{A}(k; s)$ *satisfies* IA *and* Z *if and only if there exists a sequence of weights* $w_1, \ldots, w_n$, *nonnegative and summing to* 1, *such that for all* $A = (a_{ij}) \in \mathscr{A}(n, k; s)$, $F(A) = (a_1, \ldots, a_k)$, *where* $a_j = w_1 a_{1j} + \ldots + w_n a_{nj}$.

Proof. It is easy to check that an AAM based on weighted arithmetic averaging satisfies IA and Z. Suppose, conversely, that F satisfies IA and Z. By Theorem 6.2, F satisfies SLN, and hence by Theorem 6.3 there exists a function $H: [0, s]^n \rightarrow [0, s]$ such that for all $A = (a_{ij}) \in \mathscr{A}(n, k; s), F(A) = (a_1, \ldots, a_k)$, where $a_j = H(a_{1j}, \ldots, a_{nj}), j = 1, \ldots, k$. Thus we need only show that H is a weighted arithmetic mean. Let $(\alpha_1, \ldots, \alpha_n)$ and $(\beta_1, \ldots, \beta_n)$ be members of $[0, s]^n$ such that $(\alpha_1 + \beta_1, \ldots, \alpha_n + \beta_n)$ is also a member of $[0, s]^n$, and define matrices A and $B \in \mathscr{A}(n, k; s)$ as follows: The first column of A is $[\alpha_1, \ldots, \alpha_n]^T$; the second column of A is $[\beta_1, \ldots, \beta_n]^T$; the third column of A is $[s-\alpha_1-\beta, \ldots, s-\alpha_n-\beta_n]^T$; and all other columns of A, if any, consist entirely of zeros. The first column of B is $[\alpha_1 + \beta_1, \ldots, \alpha_n + \beta_n]^T$; the third column of B is $[s-\alpha_1-\beta_1, \ldots, s-\alpha_n-\beta_n]^T$; and all other columns of B consist entirely of zeros.

By property Z, $H(0, \ldots, 0) = 0$. Thus, considering the action of H on the columns of A and B, we see that $H(\alpha_1, \ldots, \alpha_n) + H(\beta_1, \ldots, \beta_n) + H(s-\alpha_1-\beta_1, \ldots, s-\alpha_n-\beta_n) = s$, and $H(\alpha_1 + \beta_1, \ldots, \alpha_n + \beta_n) + H(s-\alpha_1-\beta_1, \ldots, s-\alpha_n-\beta_n) = s$. Hence H satisfies the multivariable Cauchy equation $H(\alpha_1 + \beta_1, \ldots, \alpha_n + \beta_n) = H(\alpha_1, \ldots, \alpha_n) + H(\beta_1, \ldots, \beta_n)$, where $a_i, \beta_i, \alpha_i + \beta_i \in [0, s]$, $i = 1, \ldots, n$.

For each $i = 1, \ldots, n$, let $h_i(\alpha) = H(0, \ldots, \alpha, \ldots, 0)$, where α occupies the i-th position in the vector $(0, \ldots, \alpha, \ldots, 0)$. It follows that $h_i(\alpha + \beta) = h_i(\alpha) + h_i(\beta)$ for all α, β such that α, β, and $\alpha + \beta \in [0, s]$.[12] Since H, and hence h, is nonnegative, it follows (Aczél [1966, p. 48, The. 3]) that there exists a nonnegative constant w_i such that $h_i(\alpha) = w_i\alpha$ for all $\alpha \in [0, s]$. But then $H(\alpha_1, \ldots, \alpha_n) = h_1(\alpha_1) + \ldots + h_n(\alpha_n) = w_1\alpha_1 + \ldots + w_n\alpha_n$. Since clearly $H(s, \ldots, s) = s$, it follows that $w_1 + \ldots + w_n = 1$, as required.

THEOREM 6.5. *An AAM* $F: \mathscr{A}(n, 2; s) \rightarrow \mathscr{A}(2; s)$ *satisfies* SLN *and* Z *if and only if there is a function* $h: [-s/2, s/2]^n \rightarrow [-s/2, s/2]$, *where*

1. h is odd $(h(-\alpha_1, \ldots, -\alpha_n) = -h(\alpha_1, \ldots, \alpha_n))$, and
2. $h(s/2, \ldots, s/2) = s/2$,

such that for all $A = (a_{ij}) \in \mathscr{A}(n, 2; s), F(A) = (a_1, a_2)$, *where* $a_j = h(a_{1j}-s/2, \ldots, a_{nj}-s/2) + s/2, j = 1, 2$.

Proof. It is easy to see that functions h satisfying 1. and 2. yield AAMs satisfying SLN and Z. Conversely, by Theorem 6.3 it follows from SLN that there exists a function $H: [0, s]^n \rightarrow [0, s]$ such that for all $A = (a_{ij}) \in \mathscr{A}(n, 2; s), F(A) = (a_1, a_2)$, where $a_j = H(a_{1j}, \ldots, a_{nj}), j = 1, 2$. By Z,

(i) $H(0, \ldots, 0) = 0$.

By considering the action of F on a matrix A whose first column is $[\alpha_1, \ldots, \alpha_n]^T$ and whose second column is $[s-\alpha_1, \ldots, s-\alpha_n]^T$, we see that

(ii) $H(\alpha_1, \ldots, \alpha_n) + H(s-\alpha_1, \ldots, s-\alpha_n) = s.$

It is easy to check (Aczél, Kannappen and Ng [to appear]) that a function H satisfies (i) and (ii) if and only if $H(\alpha_1, \ldots, \alpha_n) = h(\alpha_1 - s/2, \ldots, \alpha_n - s/2) + s/2$, where h satisfies conditions 1. and 2. specified in the present theorem.

THEOREM 6.7. *Let $\mathscr{S}$ be a tertiary σ-algebra on X and let $F: \mathscr{P}(\mathscr{S})^n \to \mathscr{P}(\mathscr{S})$ be a PAM for which there exists a function $H: [0, 1]^n \to [0, 1]$ such that $F(p_1, \ldots, p_n) = p$, where for all $A \in \mathscr{S}$, $p(A) = H(p_1(A), \ldots, p_n(A))$. Then H is a weighted arithmetic mean.*

Proof. We show that H satisfies the multivariable Cauchy equation $H(\alpha_1 + \beta_1, \ldots, \alpha_n + \beta_n) = H(\alpha_1, \ldots, \alpha_n) + H(\beta_1, \ldots, \beta_n)$, where $a_i, \beta_i, \alpha_i + \beta_i \in [0, 1]$, $i = 1, \ldots, n$, from which it follows, as in the proof of Theorem 6.4, that H is a weighted arithmetic mean. Let A_1, A_2, and A_3 be a sequence of nonempty pairwise disjoint events in $\mathscr{S}$, and choose a sequence x_1, x_2, x_3 of elements of X with $x_k \in A_k$, $k = 1, 2, 3$. Given numbers $a_i, \beta_i \in [0, 1]$ with $\alpha_i + \beta_i \in [0, 1]$, $i = 1, \ldots, n$, define a sequence of probability measures p_i, $i = 1, \ldots, n$, on $\mathscr{S}$ by $p_i(A) = \alpha_i I_1(A) + \beta_i I_2(A) + (1-\alpha_i-\beta_i) I_3(A)$, where, for $k = 1, 2, 3$, $I_k(A) = 1$ if $x_k \in A$ and $I_k(A) = 0$ if $x_k \notin A$. Then $p_i(A_1) = \alpha_i, p_i(A_2) = \beta_i$ and $p_i(A_1 \cup A_2) = \alpha_i + \beta_i$, $i = 1, \ldots, n$.

Suppose that $F(p_1, \ldots, p_n) = p$, where for all $A \in \mathscr{S}$, $p(A) = H(p_1(A), \ldots, p_n(A))$. Since p is a probability measure $p(A_1 \cup A_2) = p(A_1) + p(A_2)$, and so $H(\alpha_1 + \beta_1, \ldots, \alpha_n + \beta_n) = H(\alpha_1, \ldots, \alpha_n) + H(\beta_1, \ldots, \beta_n)$, as required.

NOTES

[1] This example is due to Aczél, Kannappan, and Ng [to appear].

[2] Our condition IA plays a role something like that of Arrow's classical condition "independence of irrelevant alternatives." But there are substantial differences in the structure and strength of the two conditions. IA is, for example, a "unary" condition, whereas Arrow's condition is "binary," in the sense that it requires a consensual ordering of two alternatives to depend only on individual orderings of these alternatives or, in recent formulations, on utilities assigned to just these alternatives. See Section 6 of this chapter for a fuller discussion.

[3] Other averaging functions, such as geometric and harmonic means and medians also fail in general, without subsequent normalization, to yield consensual values of the variables which sum to s. It was in fact this observation which led to the discovery of

earlier prototypes of Theorem 6.4, described Aczél and Wagner [1980], and Aczél, Kannappan, and Ng [to appear].

[4] Stone [1961] has called probability amalgamation methods based on weighted arithmetic averaging "opinion pools." See Sanders [1963] for applications to meteorology. An example of an aggregation method not based on arithmetic averaging is the "parimutuel method" of Eisenberg and Gale [1959]. While fascinating from a purely mathematical point of view, parimutuel consensus has been characterized by the above authors as "somewhat pathological" in actual application.

[5] For economy of exposition we have postulated the existence of the function H among the hypotheses of Theorem 6.7. A lengthier development in terms of invariance conditions analogous to IA and SLN is also possible. The present theorem is related to some interesting recent results of McConway [to appear], which deal with the class of amalgamation methods for the class of *all* σ-algebras on a set X. McConway exhibits necessary and sufficient conditions for the amalgamation methods of each class to be based on the same weighted arithmetic mean. As McConway points out, to the extent that different σ-algebras represent different assessment situations, employing the same weights in all of these situations may be undesirable. Our Theorem 6.7, which deals with a fixed σ-algebra, is a localized version of McConway's theorem which escapes the aforementioned difficulty.

It should be noted that when the probability measures in question come from a class of natural conjugate distributions, there may be good reasons for employing an amalgamation method not based on arithmetic averaging. See Winkler [1968].

[6] These authors actually state Theorem 6.9 in slightly different form since they are concerned with orderings on Euclidean n-space. Our conditions I and P allow us to translate the proof of their theorem into a proof of Theorem 6.9. The details of such translation may be found in d'Aspremont and Gevers [1977]. See also Harsanyi [1976, 1977] for an alternative axiomatization of arithmetic averaging involving certain postulates of rational behavior under risk.

[7] See Roberts [1976] or [1979] for a lucid survey of measurement theory.

[8] See, e.g., Roberts [1979, pp. 81–83].

[9] Gevers' result must be translated from the context of orderings of Euclidean space to the context of mappings of real matrices. See note 6 *supra*.

[10] By this method an individual first determines a preferential ordering of alternatives, then chooses arbitrary real numbers m and M ($m < M$) and assigns all of his most preferred alternatives the utility M and all of his least preferred alternatives the utility m. To assign a utility to an intermediate alternative he determines that probability p such that he is indifferent between getting that alternative and a lottery in which he gets a most preferred alternative with probability p, and a least preferred alternative with probability $1-p$. He then assigns the intermediate alternative the utility $(1-p)m + pM$.

[11] Characterizations of pure utilitarianism (arithmetic aggregation with all weights identical) and of Rawlsian maximin rules, appear in d'Aspremont and Gevers [1977].

[12] This technique for converting a multivariable Cauchy equation to a sequence of single variable Cauchy equations is due to Aczél, Kannappan, and Ng [to appear].

CHAPTER SEVEN

CONVERGENCE TO CONSENSUS – THE ELEMENTARY MODEL

In this chapter and the next we offer a formal account of the details of iterated arithmetic averaging and convergence to consensus. For the convenience of those who choose to read the mathematical chapters of this book (Chapters Six, Seven, and Eight) first, we include in the first section of the present chapter a brief account of the method of iterated averaging. Those who have already read Chapters Two and Three, which describe this method as applied, respectively, to the amalgamation of probabilities, and of utilities, may wish nevertheless to review the outline of this method offered in the following section. In this chapter we assume, as in Chapters Two and Three, that individuals have uniform skills at all levels of judgment. In Chapter Eight we give a formal account of iteration and convergence which deletes this assumption, thus providing a mathematical counterpart of Chapter Four.

1. ITERATED ARITHMETIC AVERAGING

Suppose that a group of n individuals is seeking consensual values of one or more numerical decision variables. In some cases these values will represent the final outcome of deliberation, as in the case of an allocation of funds among competing projects, or an assignment of probabilities to competing hypotheses. In other cases such values will play an intermediate role in some larger decision problem, as in the case of deriving a preferential ordering of a set of policy alternatives from consensual utilities assigned to these alternatives. In any case what the group requires is a method of amalgamating into a consensus individual opinions as to the most appropriate values of these decision variables.

The method which we have chosen to investigate involves the use of weighted arithmetic means as amalgamation functions. In Chapter Six we presented axiomatic characterizations of weighted arithmetic averaging as a method of producing consensual allocations (Theorem 6.4) and consensual orderings (Theorem 6.9). These characterizations pinpoint the decision problems for which arithmetic averaging is the sole rational method of amalgamating individual opinion. We recall that such strong results obtain only on the assumption that at least three decision variables are under consideration.

If fewer decision variables are involved, the justification for employing arithmetic averaging is less compelling, although some justification can be offered for such averaging in these cases on the basis of its simplicity.

In what follows we shall describe iterated arithmetic averaging for the case of a single decision variable in order to keep our notation as simple as possible. This simplification involves no loss of generality, for one may simply repeat our single variable account of iteration and convergence for as many decision variables as are involved in a given problem.

Suppose that a group of n individuals seeks consensual values of one or more decision variables. Their individual opinions as to the most appropriate values of a typical such variable are registered in a column matrix $A = [a_1, \ldots, a_n]^T$, where a_i denotes the value endorsed by individual i. Failing consensus in A the group wishes to amalgamate the opinions registered in this matrix to produce a single consensual value of the decision variable under consideration. Suppose that, based on the axiomatic characterization of weighted arithmetic averaging (Theorem 6.4) in the previous Chapter, or for reasons of simplicity, the group chooses to do this by taking a weighted arithmetic mean of the entries in A. An auxiliary decision problem then arises, namely, the determination of a consensual set of weights $w_1, \ldots, w_n$, with $0 \leqslant w_i \leqslant 1$ and $w_1 + \ldots + w_n = 1$.

Suppose that individual opinions as to the most appropriate values of these weights are registered in an $n \times n$ weight matrix $W = (w_{ij})$ where w_{ij} is the weight which i grants to j as an evaluator of the initial decision variable. By reporting the row $w_{i1}, \ldots, w_{in}$ in W individual i endorses the weighted average $a_i^{(1)} = w_{i1} a_1 + \ldots + w_{in} a_n$, an amalgamation of group opinion weighted by the expertise which he perceives that individuals bring to the task of evaluating the initial decision variable. The column matrix $A^{(1)} = WA = [a_1^{(1)}, \ldots, a_n^{(1)}]^T$ then registers the weighted averages chosen by all members of the group.

Consensus on the weights is reflected in a matrix W with identical rows. Clearly, if W is a consensus matrix, then WA is a consensus matrix, since in this case all individuals endorse the same weighted average of the entries of A. Even if W is not a consensus matrix, WA may be a consensus matrix, as shown by the following example:

$$\begin{bmatrix} 0.4 & 0.2 & 0.4 \\ 0.6 & 0.4 & 0 \\ 0.5 & 0.3 & 0.2 \end{bmatrix} \begin{bmatrix} 10 \\ 20 \\ 15 \end{bmatrix} = \begin{bmatrix} 14 \\ 14 \\ 14 \end{bmatrix}$$

Indeed, if A is already a consensus matrix, it is easy to check that for any

W, $WA = A$, so that WA is a consensus matrix. In such a case there would of course be no reason to construct W, but it is satisfying to note that consensus, once achieved, is undisturbed by weighted averaging. More generally, it is the case that any weighted average of the numbers $a_1, \ldots, a_n$ lies between the largest and smallest of these numbers. Thus weighted averaging has the desirable feature of maintaining disagreement within its original bounds.[1]

From a practical standpoint, of course, groups may be satisfied to arrive at something less than exact consensus. Let us call a matrix an ϵ-*consensus matrix* if the differences between the largest and smallest entries of each of its columns are uniformly bounded above by the positive constant ϵ. If a group reaches a state of ϵ-consensus for an agreeably small ϵ, they may very well choose to terminate their deliberations by a simple averaging of opinions, or even by a random selection from the full set of opinions. Suppose, however, that a group fails to reach a satisfactory approximation of consensus in $A^{(1)}$. The strategies of simple averaging and random selection are still available. But in such a case they tend undesirably toward expedient compromise. As we shall see below, groups need not give in so easily to such methods of resolving disagreement, for there may be other rationally superior paths to consensus.

Suppose that the column matrix of revised opinions $A^{(1)} = WA$ does not exhibit a satisfactory approximation of consensus. We wish to consider under what circumstances individuals would rationally accord the same weights to these revised opinions as they granted to the initial opinions, and thus further revise their positions from $A^{(1)}$ to $A^{(2)} = WA^{(1)}$. Now it might be asserted that such a move would be redundant, that individuals accord all of the weight which they are willing to grant to others in the move from A to $A^{(1)}$, and further multiplication by W must involve an unwarranted double weighting.

Suppose indeed that one of the members of our group of decisionmakers held this view, and thus refused to modify further his opinion registered in $A^{(1)}$. Such an individual, while according weight to the initial opinions of his colleagues registered in A accords their revised opinions in $A^{(1)}$ no weight at all. How could this be so? As argued in Chapter Two, such an individual would have to hold the view that the weights employed by his colleagues in their move from A to WA were utterly without merit. Suppose, for example, that the initial decision problem involved determining the value of some physical variable, so that the entries of W express individuals' opinions about the competence of their colleagues as physicists. An individual granting no weight to his colleagues' opinions registered in $A^{(1)}$ must believe that these colleagues are totally without competence as judges of physicists. Now there is nothing inherently contradictory in such a position, as unusual as it may seem on the basis of common experience. An individual may perceive another as being more or less skilled as a physicist than as a judge of physicists, and the above is simply an extreme case of this phenomenon which, it must be admitted, will generally result in an impasse in the decision-making process.

The foregoing example nevertheless provides a clue as to when further weighted averaging is appropriate. If each individual i, in granting the weights w_{i1}, w_{i2}, ..., w_{in} to his colleagues as evaluators of the initial decision variable, would accord them these same weights as *judges* of evaluators of that variable, then the collective move from $A^{(1)}$ to $WA^{(1)}$ is rational. Roughly speaking, one may under such circumstances view the shift from A to $A^{(1)} = WA$ as moving individual opinions to a new plateau, but one on which opinions have the same relative strengths as their counterparts in A, and thus deserve the same weight. As noted in Chapter Two, the following formal argument puts this intuition on firm ground: We originally conceived of $A^{(2)}$ as arising from repeated matrix multiplication carried out along the pattern $WA^{(1)} = W(WA)$. But by the associativity of matrix multiplication, $W(WA) = (WW)A = W^2A$. Ignore temporarily the matrix A and focus on the product W^2. The i–jth entry $w_{i1} w_{1j} + w_{i2} w_{2j} + \ldots + w_{in} w_{nj}$ of W^2 is a rational revision of the weight w_{ij} which i granted to j as, say, a physicist, since it is a weighted average of the opinions w_{1j}, w_{2j}, ..., w_{nj} on this matter, with coefficients determined by the weights w_{i1}, w_{i2}, ..., w_{in} which i has granted to individuals as judges of physicists. Hence $W^2A = A^{(2)}$ is a revision of A based on more information than the revision $A^{(1)} = WA$.

The above procedure may be iterated to the extent that individuals perceive each other as possessing uniform higher level judgmental skills. Thus if individuals are regarded as being as equally skilled judges of judges of physicists as they are judges of physicists, W^2 may also be regarded as a rational revision of weights granted to individuals as judges of physicists, and $W^2 W = W^3$ as a rational revision of weights granted to individuals as physicists. Hence, $W^3 A = WA^{(2)} = A^{(3)}$ is a rational revision of A incorporating still further information. At this stage one may perhaps begin to feel mesmerized by the staccato rhythms of "judges of judges of judges" and assert, when one's head clears, that judgments of this increasingly complex kind cannot be meaningful.[2] But the progressive modification of A by increasing powers of W does not really require that individuals assess their colleagues separately on an infinite hierarchy at judgmental skills. So long as individuals have no reason for regarding the opinions in any $A^{(n+1)} = WA^{(n)}$ as having different relative strengths than those in $A^{(n)}$, they may rationally shift to $WA^{(n+1)}$.

In such cases there arises an infinite sequence W, W^2, ... of modifications of W and a companion sequence A, WA, W^2A, ... of modifications of A. The conditions under which these sequences converge to consensus are discussed in the next two sections.

2. WEIGHT MATRICES AND HOMOGENEOUS MARKOV CHAINS

Let W be a weight matrix. We say that powers of W *converge to consensus* if there is a (necessarily unique) weight matrix L, with identical rows, such that for any $\epsilon > 0$ there exists a positive integer n_ϵ such that for all $n > n_\epsilon$, each entry of W^n differs from its counterpart in L by a number whose absolute value is less than ϵ. More informally, powers of W converge to L if the entries of sufficiently large powers of W lie as close as we like to their counterparts in L. It is clear that if the sequence of powers W^1, W^2, ... converges to the consensus matrix L, then the companion sequence of modifications of A, WA, W^2A, ... also converges to a consensus matrix with the dimensions of A.

There is a rich body of literature on matrices with nonnegative entries and unit row sums. The initial interest in such matrices arose in probability theory, where matrices of this kind define a stochastic process known as a *finite homogeneous Markov chain*. Here the entries of a matrix express certain conditional probabilities, and convergence theorems are stated in probabilistic language. Since the formal mathematical structure underlying the theory of Markov chains is identical to that of the theory of weight matrices, one may translate the theorems of Markov chain theory into the language of weights and consensus. When this translation is carried out, one discovers may intuitively appealing concepts related to group decisionmaking as counterparts of more traditional probabilistic concepts.[3]

As we shall see in Chapter Eight, however, the perspective of group decisionmaking and consensus raises some convergence questions for products of arbitrary weight matrices which probability theorists have had no reason to investigate.

3. CONVERGENCE TO CONSENSUS

Given a weight matrix $W = (w_{ij})$ let us say that individual i *respects individual j* if the weight w_{ij} which i grants to j is positive ($w_{ij} > 0$). In particular, if $w_{ii} > 0$, we say that i *respects himself*. Now suppose that every individual respects himself, and every other individual as well, so that all of the entries of W are positive. A classical theorem of the theory of Markov chains guarantees that in such a case the sequence $W, W^2, \ldots$ converges to consensus:

THEOREM 7.1. *Let $W = (w_{ij})$ be a weight matrix with exclusively positive entries. Then there is a unique weight matrix L with identical rows and exclusively positive entries such that powers of W converge to L. Moreover, the entries $\lambda_1, \ldots, \lambda_n$ comprising each row of L are the unique solution to the simultaneous linear equations*

$$(x_1, \ldots, x_n) W = (x_1, \ldots, x_n)$$
$$x_1 + \ldots + x_n = 1.$$

A proof of the foregoing theorem appears in Kemeny and Snell [1976]. Although this theorem states by no means the most general conditions under which convergence to consensus occurs, it is of substantial interest in demonstrating that a not uncommon pattern of respect among individuals gives rise to convergence to consensus in which each person's initial opinion is granted some positive consensual weight. The theorem tells us, moreover, that the consensual weights $\lambda_1, \ldots, \lambda_n$ derived from iterated averaging can be calculated from W by solving a set of simultaneous equations. These weights simply comprise the unique "fixed point weight vector" associated to W. Hence no computation of powers of W is required in order to determine the consensual weights.

Even if an individual i assigns an individual j the weight $w_{ij} = 0$ in W, he may revise this assignment to a positive weight in W^2, in virtue of respecting some individual k who respects j. This observation suggests that one might expect powers of W to converge to consensus under a much broader set of conditions than those described in Theorem 7.1. Let us say that there is a *chain of respect from individual i to individual j* if there is some sequence of individuals, beginning with i and ending with j, such that each individual in the sequence respects the individual listed directly after him in the sequence. The length of a chain of respect is defined to be one less than the number of individuals listed (with repetitions of any individual included in the count), and counts thereby the number of links in the chain.

It is easy to show by induction that there is a chain of respect from i to j of length r precisely when the i–jth element $w_{ij}^{(r)}$ of W^r is positive. There is thus a simple algorithm for confirming the existence of a chain of respect of length r. Now suppose that there is at least one individual k such that there is a chain of respect from every other individual to k (and, hence, from k to himself). Another well known theorem of the theory of Markov chains guarantees that if k, or any similarly respected individual, respects himself, then powers of W converge to consensus:

THEOREM 7.2. *Let W be a weight matrix and let E denote the set of all individuals k for which there is a chain of respect from every other individual to k. If E is nonempty and at least one member of E respects himself, then powers of W converge to a weight matrix L with identical rows. The entries $\lambda_1, \ldots, \lambda_n$ comprising each row of L are the unique solution to the simultaneous linear equations*

$$(x_1, \ldots, x_n) W = (x_1, \ldots, x_n)$$
$$x_1 + \ldots + x_n = 1,$$

and an individual i receives positive consensual weight ($\lambda_i > 0$) if and only if i belongs to E.

The proof of Theorem 7.2 follows immediately from a theorem of Doob [1953, p. 173].[4] Note that under the conditions stated in this theorem some members of the group may receive a consensual weight of zero. Such individuals consent to be excluded from the decisionmaking process by granting to others respect which is not reciprocated and by persisting in this respect at higher levels with the full knowledge of how these others have evaluated them at lower levels. As in the case of Theorem 7.1 consensual weights may be calculated on the basis of W alone simply by solving a set of simultaneous linear equations.

We may paraphrase Theorem 7.2 as follows: If there is at least one individual k for which there is a chain of respect from every other individual to k, then powers of W fail to converge to consensus only if no such individual k respects himself. We would of course expect in general that all individuals in the group (or at least all those who occupy a position at the end of a chain of respect emanating from every other individual) would grant themselves positive weight in W. But modesty or some predetermined convention that everyone is to assign himself an initial weight of zero may result in a situation where convergence to consensus fails to obtain despite the linking of the group by an individual to whom everyone communicates respect via some chain of respect. We claim that in such situations, despite the failure of convergence of powers of W to consensus, there is a unique rational consensual set of weights implicit in the patterns of respect incorporated in W.

For suppose that W is a weight matrix for which there is at least one individual k such that there is a chain of respect from every individual to k.

Choose any ϵ such that $0 < \epsilon < 1$ and let W_ϵ denote the weight matrix derived from W by adding ϵ to each of the diagonal elements of W and adjusting the rows of the resulting matrix so that all row sums are unitary and the ratio of any two non-diagonal elements in any row is equal to the ratio of the corresponding elements of W.

In algebraic terms, this amounts to setting $W_\epsilon = \epsilon I + (1-\epsilon)W$, where I is the $n \times n$ matrix with ones on the main diagonal and zeros in every other position. By choosing ϵ sufficiently small, the elements of W_ϵ may be made to lie as close as we like to their counterparts in W. Now any such W_ϵ has positive entries wherever W has positive entries. Hence all the chains of respect defined by W are also chains of respect defined by W_ϵ. In particular, for W_ϵ there is also at least one individual k such that there is a chain of respect from every other individual to k. In addition, all of the diagonal elements of W_ϵ are positive, i.e., everyone respect himself in W_ϵ. Hence by Theorem 7.2 powers of W_ϵ converge to a weight matrix L with identical rows $\lambda_1, \ldots, \lambda_n$, where $(\lambda_1, \ldots, \lambda_n)$ is the unique fixed point weight vector of W_ϵ, i.e., the unique solution of the simultaneous linear equations

$$(x_1, \ldots, x_n) \, W_\epsilon = (x_1, \ldots, x_n)$$
$$x_1 + \ldots + x_n = 1.$$

We propose that the group adopt $\lambda_1, \ldots, \lambda_n$ as a consensual set of weights, letting W_ϵ "stand in," as it were, for W. Now it appears on the surface that these weights depend on ϵ, casting doubt on how well defined these consensual weights are. But it may be shown that for *any* ϵ with $0 < \epsilon < 1$, powers of W_ϵ converge to the same consensus matrix. The key to seeing this is to notice that for any ϵ, the fixed point weight vectors of W_ϵ are identical with those of W.[5] *Hence the unique fixed point weight vector of each W_ϵ is equal to what is now revealed to be the unique fixed point weight vector of W.* Thus each W_ϵ possesses the same unique fixed point weight vector and powers of each W_ϵ converge to the same matrix L with identical rows λ_1, $\ldots, \lambda_n$, where $(\lambda_1, \ldots, \lambda_n)$ is the unique fixed point weight vector of W. As in the case of Theorem 7.2 consensual weights may once again be extracted directly from W. We may combine Theorem 7.2 with the above remark into one summary convergence theorem:

THEOREM 7.3. *Let W be a weight matrix and let E denote the set of all individuals k such that there is a chain of respect from every other individual to k. If E is nonempty, then* (1) *powers of W converge to consensus, or* (2) *for each ϵ with $0 < \epsilon < 1$, powers of $W_\epsilon = \epsilon I + (1-\epsilon)W$ converge to consensus* *independently of ϵ. In each case the consensual weights $\lambda_1, \ldots, \lambda_n$ constitute the unique fixed point weight vector of W and individual i receives positive consensual weight ($\lambda_i > 0$) if and only if i belongs to E.*

We emphasize again that under the hypotheses of Theorem 7.3, powers of W fail to converge to consensus only in the unlikely case that no member of E respects himself. Whether this comes about through modesty or convention, the move to "substitute" some W_ϵ for W in such a case can hardly be objectionable, for our discussion preceding Theorem 7.3 demonstrates that the modesty or convention which results in each person in E assigning himself the weight zero in W is expressed in fully equivalent fashion by having each such person assign himself some identical positive weight, and maintaining the ratios between the weights he assigns to other people.

4. SOME CONSENSUAL WEIGHT CALCULATIONS

We now compute the unique fixed point weight vectors of a number of matrices satisfying the hypotheses of Theorem 7.3 in order to convey some feeling for the nature of the consensus which emerges from iterated averaging.

Consider first the case of a symmetric $n \times n$ weight matrix W, i.e., one in which for all individuals i and j, i grants the same weight to j as j grants to i ($w_{ij} = w_{ji}$). It is easy to check that $(1/n, \ldots, 1/n)$ is always a fixed point weight vector for any such matrix. Moreover, if W satisfies the respect hypothesis of Theorem 7.3, then $(1/n, \ldots, 1/n)$ is the unique fixed point weight vector of W. In such cases each individual receives the same consensual weight, and aggregation of the values which they assign to the initial decision variables is performed by simple arithmetic averaging. Note that the entries of each column of a symmetric weight matrix sum to one. One checks easily that it is in virtue of this property that $(1/n, \ldots, 1/n)$ is a fixed point weight vector of any symmetric weight matrix. More generally it is easy to show that $(1/n, \ldots, 1/n)$ is a fixed point weight vector of W if and only if the entries of each column of W sum to one. Hence for matrices W satisfying the respect hypothesis of Theorem 7.3, the unique fixed point weight vector of W is $(1/n, \ldots, 1/n)$ if and only if the entries in each column of W sum to one. Thus each individual receives the same consensual weight by iterated averaging if and only if the weights granted to each person (as well as by each person) sum to a full unit vote. This elegant and intuitively appealing result should contribute to dispelling some of the initial mystery surrounding iterated averaging. The remaining examples in this section, supplemented by the non-iterative approach to consensus described in the next section, will reveal further the naturalness and simplicity of the matrix model of consensus.

Let us consider next the case of an arbitrary 2×2 weight matrix

$$W = \begin{vmatrix} 1-w_{12} & w_{12} \\ w_{21} & 1-w_{21} \end{vmatrix}.$$

Such a matrix satisfies the respect hypothesis of Theorem 7.3 if and only if at least one of the quantities w_{12} or w_{21} is positive. In such a case, the unique fixed point weight vector of W is (λ_1, λ_2), where $\lambda_1 = w_{21}/(w_{12} + w_{21})$ and $\lambda_2 = w_{12}/(w_{12} + w_{21})$. Hence the consensual weight accorded an individual is directly proportional to the initial weight granted him by his colleague.

There are weight matrices satisfying the respect hypothesis of Theorem 7.3 having remarkably few positive entries. Consider, for example, the $n \times n$ matrix W in which each individual i grants himself the positive weight $1-q_i$ and individual $i + 1$ (or 1, if $i = n$), the positive weight q_i. For such matrices the consensual weight received by individual i is $\lambda_i = (1/q_i) / (1/q_1 + \ldots + 1/q_n)$. Note that $\lambda_i/\lambda_j = q_j/q_i$ so that if, for example, i proxies away twice the weight proxied away by j, he will receive half the consensual weight received by j. Note that the 2×2 example considered above is a special case of the present example. The reader may also confirm that if in the present example W is modified off its main diagonal by having each individual assign the identical weight $q_i/n-1$ to every other individual, then the same set of consensual weights emerges.

The reader will find additional calculations of weights in a concrete numerical setting in Chapter Two. In that chapter actual matrix powers are calculated to illustrate graphically how consensus emerges by iteration.

5. THE CENTRAL ROLE OF FIXED POINT WEIGHT MATRICES

We have already observed in Section 3 that a weight matrix has a unique fixed point weight vector if there is at least one individual k such that there is a chain of respect from every other individual to k. Under this hypothesis we have endorsed this unique fixed point weight vector as the rational consensual set of weights implicit in W, arguing (by Theorem 7.3) that then powers of W or of some innocuous modification of W converge to a matrix with rows identically equal to that fixed point vector.

Now it turns out that the connection between the respect hypothesis of Theorem 7.3 and the existence of a unique fixed point weight vector is even stronger than that noted above:

THEOREM 7.4. *The weight matrix W has a unique fixed point weight vector if and only if the weights in W are such that there is at least one individual k such that there is a chain of respect from every other individual to k.*

The proof of this theorem follows from a more general theorem in Berman and Plemmons [1979, p. 244] to which we shall again allude in the next section. The special case represented by Theorem 7.4, asserts that a respect condition on the basis of which it is natural to expect consensus to emerge is equivalent to the existence of a unique fixed point weight vector. This strong correspondence suggests that one might give an argument for employing that fixed point weight vector as the consensual set of weights without reference to the fact that some sequence of matrix powers converges to a matrix with rows identically equal to that fixed point vector. We think that there is a convincing non-iterative argument on behalf of this claim. To the extent that one is convinced by our argument, one can, if one is so inclined, then view iterated weighting and convergence to consensus in more metaphorical fashion. We emphasize, however, that whether one inclines toward the iterative account already presented, or toward the non-iterative point of view described below, one arrives at the identical set of consensual weights.

To make our argument concrete let us suppose that in the initial decision problem, the value of some physical variable is in question and individual opinions as to the most appropriate value of this variable are given by the column matrix $A = [a_1, \ldots, a_n]^T$. Now suppose that each person regards every person in the group as having uniform (though perhaps individually differing) skills as a physicist and as a judge of physicists. Suppose further that (1) this uniformity of judgmental skills is perceived to persist at all higher levels, as in the iterative account described in Section 1; or (2) individuals are simply unable to assess levels of judgment beyond the second. In either case there are no higher order weights which differ from the identical weights which individuals assign at the first two levels. All of the information available is then contained in a single weight matrix $W = (w_{ij})$ where w_{ij} is the weight which i grants to j, both as a physicist and as a judge of physicists.

We seek a consensual set of weights $\lambda_1, \ldots, \lambda_n$ with which to average the entries in A. Suppose that $\lambda_1, \ldots, \lambda_n$ is such a proposed set of weights, based on the attributions of respect in W. Adoption of this set of weights would result in the adoption of $(\lambda_1, \ldots, \lambda_n)A = \lambda_1 a_1 + \ldots + \lambda_n a_n$ as the consensual value of the initial decision variable. On the other hand, since individuals are perceived to have uniform skills as physicists and as judges of physicists, this same set of weights are appropriate weights with which to average the columns of W (regarded as a first order weight matrix) to produce consensual evaluations of individuals as physicists. But then the row vector $(\lambda_1, \ldots, \lambda_n)W$ is a competitor with $(\lambda_1, \ldots, \lambda_n)$ as the appropriate set of weights with which to average the columns of A.

Hence if $\lambda_1, \ldots, \lambda_n$ is an appropriate set of weights with which to average the columns of A, consistency requires that

$$(\lambda_1, \ldots, \lambda_n)A = (\lambda_1, \ldots, \lambda_n)WA$$

for all possible column vectors A. It follows[6] that any reasonable set of weights must satisfy the relation

$$(\lambda_1, \ldots, \lambda_n)W = (\lambda_1, \ldots, \lambda_n),$$

that is, any candidate for a consensual set of weights must be a fixed point weight vector of W. Now every weight matrix has either an infinite number of fixed vectors (see the next section of this chapter) or a unique fixed point weight vector. In the former case there is no clear choice of a consensual set of weights (we offer speculations on how to handle such cases in the next section). In the latter case, which according to Theorem 7.4, occurs precisely when a respect condition is fulfilled that leads one to expect that there is *some* reasonable set of consensual weights implicit in W, there is but a single reasonable candidate for this set of weights, namely the unique fixed point weight vector of W.[7]

The above argument can be stretched even a little further. Suppose that individuals evaluate each other as physicists in the weight matrix W and have no information on the basis of which they can assess any higher level judgmental skills. If W has a unique fixed point weight vector, we would in this situation endorse that vector as the reasonable set of consensual weights with which to average the entries of A. The only obvious alternatives to this decision are (1) to endorse no consensus in this case or (2) to compromise with simple arithmetic averaging of the columns of W to produce consensual weights. The latter move implicitly attributes equal skills to all as judges of physicists, whereas our approach implicitly attributes the same weights to individuals as judges of physicists as they are granted as physicists. We recognize that individuals who reject alternative (1) above may have differing inclinations about how to resolve dissensus in W. We of course do not reject (2) if the individuals in the decisionmaking group are in agreement that each deserves the same weight as a judge of physicists. But failing any perceptions of this kind of their part, it seems most reasonable to us to assume that their skills as judges of physicists are more likely to be approximated by the weights in W than by equal weights.

6. CONSENSUS FOR ARBITRARY WEIGHT MATRICES

For weight matrices W satisfying the respect hypothesis of Theorem 7.3 we have offered both an iterative and a non-iterative justification for regarding the unique fixed point weight vector of W as the rational consensual set of weights implicit in W. This respect hypothesis amounts to the assumption that E is nonempty, where E consists of all those individuals k such that there is a chain of respect from every individual in the group to k. Under the circumstances there is a chain of respect from every individual in E to every other individual in E, but no chain of respect from any individual in E to any individual outside E. The entire group thus splits into two disjoint subgroups, E and its complement, which we denote by T. If we list all r members of E first, followed by the $n-r$ members of T, the weight matrix W in this situation takes the block form

$$W = \left[\begin{array}{c|c} W_E & 0 \\ \hline W_T & \end{array} \right],$$

where W_E is $r \times r$, 0 is the $r \times (n-r)$ matrix consisting entirely of zeros and W_T is $(n-r) \times n$. Under the above assumptions W_E possesses a unique fixed point weight vector $(\lambda_1, \ldots, \lambda_r)$ with exclusively positive entries and W has the unique fixed point vector $(\lambda_1, \ldots, \lambda_r, 0, 0, \ldots, 0)$. If at least one individual in E grants himself positive weight then powers of W converge to a matrix with rows identically equal to $(\lambda_1, \ldots, \lambda_r, 0, 0, \ldots, 0)$.

Now the original group may very well be more fragmented in its patterns of respect then the group described above. It is easy to see that an arbitrary weight matrix W gives rise to a partition of individuals into subgroups E_1, $E_2, \ldots, E_m$ and T, where for each E_i there is a chain of respect from every individual in E_i to every other individual in E_i and no chain of respect from any individual in E_i to any individual in E_j ($j \neq i$) or to any individual in T. From every individual in T, there is a chain of respect to at least one individual outside T.[8] Listing all members of E_1 first, then those of E_2, etc. the weight matrix W in this case takes the block form

$$W = \begin{bmatrix} \begin{array}{c|c} \begin{matrix} W_{E_1} & & \\ & W_{E_2} & & 0 \\ 0 & & \\ & & W_{E_m} \end{matrix} & 0 \\ \hline & W_T & \end{array} \end{bmatrix}$$

Now corresponding to each submatrix W_{E_i} there is a unique fixed point weight vector of W with positive weights assigned to all individuals in E_i and zero weight to all individuals outside E_i. And the full set of fixed point weight vectors for W is generated by taking linear combinations, with coefficients nonnegative and summing to one, of these special fixed point weight vectors. (See Berman and Plemmons [1979, p. 224]) Within each of the subgroups E_i there is consensus regarding the assignment of weights and the special fixed point weight vector derived from each E_i as described above summarizes that consensus. When $m \geq 2$ the group as a whole exhibits dissensus. If consensus of the entire group is required on practical grounds, we would suggest in this case that a reasonable choice of a set of consensual weights is that linear combination of the special fixed point weight vectors attached to each E_i whose coefficients are proportional to the number of members in each subgroup. This proposal amounts to a procedure of first ascertaining any partial consensus implicit in W, and then employing as a democratic expedient, simple averaging over the consensual weight vectors endorsed by members of the subgroups $E_1, \ldots, E_m$. As in the case where $m = 1$, members of T receive a consensual weight of zero by this method.

7. CHOOSING WEIGHTS

In the preceding discussion we have regarded weights, in neutral fashion, simply as parts of a unit vote. We now consider the question of how weights might be chosen. It is clear that the answer to this question will vary with the decisionmaking situation at hand, so that no universally applicable approach to the choice of weights should be expected. In certain cases groups may have extensive statistical information on the past performance of their members. In other cases judgments of reliability may be highly subjective. The following examples illustrate the complexity and diversity of the problem of choosing weights:

1. *An elementary census problem.* Suppose that n individuals are given a

collection of N objects, each bearing a label from the set $\{1, 2, \ldots, k\}$, and must determine the fraction p_j of objects bearing the label j for each $j = 1, 2, \ldots, k$. Suppose further that the collection is partitioned into n disjoint subsets, and that individual i examines a subset with N_i objects and reports, for each $j = 1, 2, \ldots, k$, the fraction p_{ij} of objects in that set which bear the label j. The $n \times k$ matrix $A = (p_{ij})$ will only rarely exhibit consensus. But the rational sequence of weights $w_1, w_2, \ldots, w_n$ with which to average the columns of A is immediately apparent. Individual i should receive a weight proportional to the size of the set which he examines, so that $w_i = N_i/N$. For assuming that individuals count correctly, it is easy to check that $p_j = w_1 p_{1j} + w_2 p_{2j} + \ldots + w_n p_{nj}$ correctly reports the fraction of objects in the entire set which bear the label j. Artificial as this simple combinatorial exercise may be, it illustrates in pure form the type of decision problem in which deliberative responsibility is partitioned in such a way that committee reports are accorded full credibility but weighted to reflect the scope of their unique concerns.

2. *Estimation with minimal variance.* Suppose that n individuals are attempting with unbiased devices of differing accuracy to measure a quantity μ. Assume further that their estimates $a_1, \ldots, a_n$ of this number may be regarded as realizations of a sequence of independent random variables $X_1, \ldots, X_n$, with variances σ_i^2. Variances are often used as "performance" measures in estimation problems, reliability varying inversely with variance magnitude. If this measure of reliability is adopted by the group, the group should adopt as their consensual estimate of μ the number $w_1 a_1 + \ldots + w_n a_n$, where the weights w_i are chosen to minimize the variance σ^2 of the random variable $w_1 X_1 + \ldots + w_n X_n$. It is easy to check that $\sigma^2 = w_1^2 \sigma_1^2 + \ldots + w_n^2 \sigma_n^2$, and a little partial differentiation then shows that σ^2 is minimized when $w_i = (1/\sigma_i^2)/(1/\sigma_1^2 + \ldots + 1/\sigma_n^2)$. In decision-making contexts like the one under discussion, one might initially have been inclined to endorse the estimate of the individual with smallest variance as the rational group estimate. Yet such a policy is demonstrably inferior (with respect to variance minimization) to the use of the above weighted average, indicating the wisdom of collective deliberation on a single matter, even when some individuals are more expert at this matter than others.

3. *Consensual weather forecasting.* Sanders [1963] describes a measure of performance based on an individual's past probabilistic predictions of mete-orological events. This "verification score," expressed as an average over N

forecasts, is given by by $F = ((f_1 - 0_1)^2 + \ldots + (f_n - 0_n)^2)/N$, where f_i is the forecast probability and 0_i the "observed" probability, which is assigned the value one if the event occurs and zero if it does not. Here perfectly correct and completely confident forecasting receives a score of zero and its extreme opposite a score of one. This verification score can of course be computed for a sequence of consensual probability forecasts as well, and Sanders offers empirical evidence that a consensus of probabilities based on even simple arithmetic averaging can attain a verification score better than that of any individual contributing to the consensus. While Sanders did not investigate weighted averaging it is clear that such a refinement is possible. The question of how to extract weights, perhaps from individual verification scores, in order to minimize the score of consensual prediction is a matter for empirical investigation.

4. *Magnitude estimation.* When a decision problem involves neither highly structured estimation subject to a priori analysis of weighting schemes, as in examples 1 and 2 above, nor a statistical record of past performance, as in the preceding example, then the choice of weights becomes a subjective enterprise. In such cases decisionmakers have sometimes found it useful to approach the problem of quantification by a method known as "magnitude estimation." Roberts [1979] describes the use of this method in assigning ratings of relative importance for energy demand to eleven variables related to commuter bus transportation in a given region. By this method, an individual selects that variable which seems most important and assigns it the rating 100. He then rates the other variables by comparison to the most important one, so that a variable receiving a rating of 50 is considered "half as important" as one receiving a rating of 100, etc. Individuals, particularly after some experience, are apparently comfortable making such estimates.

The method of magnitude estimation might thus provide a useful approach to choosing weights in subjective contexts. An individual would rank his colleagues, as described above, assigning ratings that reflect their relative expertise. Weights would then by extracted by normalizing the ratings.[9]

NOTES

[1] While the individual weighted averages $a_1^{(1)}, \ldots, a_n^{(1)}$ of the numbers $a_1, \ldots, a_n$ all lie between the largest and smallest of these numbers, they may have greater variance than the numbers $a_1, \ldots, a_n$.

[2] In Section 5 of this chapter we offer a non-iterative account of consensus which yields

the same consensual weights as those derived (see Sections 2 and 3) from convergence of the iterative procedure now under discussion.

[3] French [1956] and Harary [1959] appear to be the first to have suggested Markov Chains as a (descriptive) model of group decisionmaking. On their view the weights were power parameters and iteration was seen to represent diachronically the repeated episodes of force, resistance, and acquiescence involved in the manifestations of social power. De Groot [1974] appears to be the first to have endorsed Markov Chains as a normative model of consensus. In his brief treatment, however, no justification for iteration is offered.

[4] This theorem asserts that powers of W converge to consensus if and only if some power W^r has a column j with all entries positive. The foregoing condition corresponds, by our remarks preceding Theorem 7.2, to the existence of a chain of respect of length r from every individual in the group (including individual j) to j. Now the hypothesis of Theorem 7.2 specifying that E be nonempty, while it implies the existence of chains of respect from every individual to j, does not guarantee that they will have some common length r. The additional hypothesis that at least one member of E respects himself enables one to show the existence of such chains by inserting repetitions of that individual's name in a given set of chains to bring them up to some uniform length. We remark that the convergence of powers of W to consensus is decidable, for Isaacson and Madsen (1974) have shown that if some power of an $n \times n$ weight matrix W has a column with exclusively positive entries, then the power $W^{n2-3n+3}$ has a column with exclusively positive entries.

[5] Suppose that $(\lambda_1, \ldots, \lambda_n)W = (\lambda_1, \ldots, \lambda_n)$. Then $(\lambda_1, \ldots, \lambda_n)(\epsilon I + (1-\epsilon)W) = \epsilon(\lambda_1, \ldots, \lambda_n) + (1-\epsilon)(\lambda_1, \ldots, \lambda_n)W = \epsilon(\lambda_1, \ldots, \lambda_n) + (1-\epsilon)(\lambda_1, \ldots, \lambda_n) = (\lambda_1, \ldots, \lambda_n)$. On the other hand, if $(\lambda_1, \ldots, \lambda_n)(\epsilon I + (1-\epsilon)W) = (\lambda_1, \ldots, \lambda_n)$, then $\epsilon(\lambda_1, \ldots, \lambda_n) + (1-\epsilon)(\lambda_1, \ldots, \lambda_n)W = (\lambda_1, \ldots, \lambda_n)$. Hence, $(1-\epsilon)(\lambda_1, \ldots, \lambda_n)W = (1-\epsilon)(\lambda_1, \ldots, \lambda_n)$, and so $(\lambda_1, \ldots, \lambda_n)W = (\lambda_1, \ldots, \lambda_n)$.

[6] Of course, if the relation $(\lambda_1, \ldots, \lambda_n)A = (\lambda_1, \ldots, \lambda_n)WA$ holds for just a single column vector A, we may not be able to "cancel" the A's to derive the relation $(\lambda_1, \ldots, \lambda_n) = (\lambda_1, \ldots, \lambda_n)W$. In general, however, the set of possible column vectors A that might arise is extensive enough to include a linearly independent set of n such vectors, from which it follows by elementary linear algebra that $(\lambda_1, \ldots, \lambda_n)W = (\lambda_1, \ldots, \lambda_n)$.

[7] Someone might ask whether a fixed point vector of W^2 would not be better than a fixed point vector of W in this respect, since W^2 contains "more information" then W. But it is easy to see on the basis of the discussion in the next section that the fixed point vectors of W are identical with those of any power of W.

[8] In classical Markov Chain terminology the sets E_j are the *ergodic classes* and T is the class of *transient states*.

[9] Saaty (1977) has proposed the following elaboration on the method of magnitude estimation: An individual constructs a matrix $R = (r_{ij})$ of weight ratios, where r_{ij} is an estimate of w_i/w_j. The entries are subject only to the restriction $r_{ij} = 1/r_{ji}$. Weights are extracted from this matrix as entries of the normalized eigenvector corresponding to the largest real positive eigenvalue of R. The r_{ij} are not assumed to satisfy the consistency condition $r_{ij} r_{jk} = r_{ik}$. If this condition is satisfied, then the columns of R are scalar multiples of each other and weights are determined by normalizing any column of R.

CHAPTER EIGHT

CONVERGENCE TO CONSENSUS – THE EXTENDED MODEL

In the preceding chapter we examined an elementary model of group decisionmaking in which a single set of individuals evaluated both the initial decision variable at issue and each others' expertise at this and higher order judgmental tasks. Our analysis was carried out under the assumption that individuals were perceived to have uniform, though perhaps individually differing, skills at all of the relevant levels of judgment. In this setting consensus, when it was implicit in the pattern of respect among members of the group, emerged as the limit of powers of a single square weight matrix.

In this chapter we consider an extended model of group decisionmaking for which the restrictive assumptions of the elementary model are deleted. The present chapter is thus a formal counterpart of Chapter Four. Our ultimate extension of the elementary model is actually a threefold generalization of that model in that it deletes (1) the assumption of uniform weights at all levels, (2) the assumption that a single set of individuals carries out all of the relevant evaluative tasks, and (3) the assumption that iterated averaging involves arithmetic means. So as not to burden the reader initially with too much generality, we describe first the extension to the case of non-uniform weights, maintaining the assumptions of a single group of decisionmakers and arithmetic averaging. After describing convergence to consensus in this setting, we sketch a variant of this analysis which accommodates the possibility that different groups may be responsible for evaluation at different levels. In a final section on what we call *quasi-arithmetic averaging functions* we show how the convergence of matrix products is relevant to consensus involving iterated averaging of a very general sort. In this extension of the elementary model, ·matrix products arise not only through iterated arithmetic averaging, but also by iteration of any of an infinite class of averaging functions including weighted geometric and harmonic means. With this ultimate generalization of the elementary model we rest our case for the cogency of matrix models of consensus.

1. A SIMPLE EXTENSION OF THE ELEMENTARY MODEL

Suppose, as in the preceding chapter, that a group of n individuals seeks consensual values of some numerical decision variable. Their individual opinions as to the most appropriate value of this variable are registered in a column matrix $A = [a_1, \ldots, a_n]^T$. Failing consensus in A, the group constructs an $n \times n$ weight matrix W_1, the $i-j$th entry of which expresses the respect of individual i for individual j in the matter of evaluating the initial decision variable. Failing consensus in $W_1 A$, the group constructs a weight matrix W_2, the $i-j$th entry of which expresses the respect of individual i for individual j as a judge of evaluators of the initial decision variable. Iteration of this procedure may lead in theory to a sequence W_1, W_2, ... of weight matrices each expressing an evaluation of individuals at some level in a hierarchy of judgmental skills. There is no assumption of equality between any of these matrices. In this case the sequence of powers W, W^2, ... and its companion sequence A, WA, WA^2, ... arising in the elementary model is replaced by a sequence of products W_1, $W_2 W_1$, ... and a companion sequence A, $W_1 A$, $W_2 W_1 A$, ... As in the elementary case, if the sequence W_1, $W_2 W_1$, ... approaches as a limit a weight matrix with identical rows (i.e., if W_1, $W_2 W_1$, ... converges to consensus) then, for any A, the sequence A, $W_1 A$, $W_2 W_1 A$, ... converges to consensus. Hence we wish to find conditions under which a sequence of products of weight matrices converges to consensus, since the patterns of respect expressed in such weight matrices yield consensus on the value of the initial decision variable, regardless of the initial state of disagreement about this issue.

We consider first a simple variant of the elementary model where there is some level m, such that for all levels $i \geqslant m$, the weight matrices W_i are identically equal to some matrix W. In this situation individuals may be perceived to have non-uniform judgmental skills at the first $m-1$ levels, but at level m and all higher levels they are perceived to have uniform judgmental skills. This is the situation which one expects to find most often in practice, in most cases with $m = 2$ or $m = 3$. It is obvious that if powers of W converge to consensus, then the sequence of matrix products W_1, $W_2 W_1$, ... does likewise:

THEOREM 8.1. *Let W_1, W_2, ... be a sequence of weight matrices for which there is some level m and some weight matrix W such that for all levels $i \geqslant m$, $W_i = W$. Then if powers of W converge to a matrix with rows identically equal to $[\lambda_1, \ldots, \lambda_n]$, the sequence W_1, $W_2 W_1$, ... converges to a matrix with rows identically equal to $[\lambda_1, \ldots, \lambda_n] W_{m-1} \ldots W_1$.*

In particular, if W satisfies the respect hypotheses stated in Theorem 7.2, the sequence of matrix products, W_1, $W_2 W_1$, ... converges to consensus.

Suppose that powers of W do not converge to consensus. We would propose to treat this situation exactly as we treated it in the case of the elementary model:

(1) If there is at least one individual k such that W defines a chain of respect from every individual to k, i.e., if W has a unique fixed point weight vector $[\lambda_1, \ldots, \lambda_n]$, then $[\lambda_1, \ldots, \lambda_n] W_{m-1} \ldots W_1$ is the rational set of weights with which to average the entries of A, for the same reasons as those advanced in the discussion preceding Theorem 7.3, and in the alternative non-iterative account described in Section 5 of chapter 7. Moreover, based on the same arguments as those offered in that section, we would endorse the above set of weights as the rational consensual choice, even if individuals construct no weight matrices beyond W_m.

(2) Suppose that W is such that the group is fragmented into subgroups in the manner described in Section 7 of chapter 7, so that there are an infinite number of fixed point weight vectors. We would again choose, as a democratic expedient, that fixed point weight vector $[\lambda_1, \ldots, \lambda_n]$ which is a linear combination of the special fixed point vectors associated to each subgroup, with coefficients proportional to subgroup size, and endorse $[\lambda_1, \ldots, \lambda_n] W_{m-1}$ $\ldots W_1$ as the appropriate set of weights with which to average the entries of A.

2. CONVERGENCE OF PRODUCTS OF ARBITRARY WEIGHT MATRICES

In the above section we treated that case of the extended model most likely to arise in practice. It is of some theoretical interest, however, to describe some conditions under which products of weight matrices from an arbitrary infinite sequence converge to consensus. We give by no means a complete account of such convergence conditions, limiting ourselves to the exposition and proof of a few interesting cases which point up special features of the extended model and yet illustrate the breadth of conditions under which convergence occurs.

As an illustration of the subtleties of the extended model, let us consider how to generalize the convergence criterion in Theorem 7.1, which asserts that if all entries of W are positive, then powers of W converge to consensus. In the elementary model, the exact magnitude of a weight granted by one individual to another is, so long as it is positive, not relevant to the presence or absence of convergence. Magnitudes do, of course, influence rates of convergence, as well as the nature of the consensual limit. But the fact of convergence or the lack thereof is determined simply by the pattern of positive entries in W.

In the more general case of products of arbitrary weight matrices the magnitudes of weights are explicitly relevant to the issue of convergence. It is *not* the case that if every matrix in the sequence W_1, W_2, ... has exclusively positive entries, then the sequence of products W_1, $W_2 W_1$, ... converges to consensus. Theorem 7.1 generalizes to the extended model in a less comprehensive way.

We need to regard the positivity of all elements of a fixed matrix W in a slightly different way in order to discover a viable generalization of Theorem 7.1. Consider, then, a matrix W with exclusively positive entries. Let us denote by μ the smallest entry of W, so that $w_{ij} \geqslant \mu > 0$ for each entry w_{ij} of W. The number μ constitutes a positive lower bound (however small) on the respect which individuals accord themselves and their colleagues at all levels of judgment. This property of minimal positive respect may be formulated for an arbitrary sequence of weight matrices and, in fact, insures convergence of products of these matrices to consensus:

THEOREM 8.2. *Let W_1, W_2, ... be a sequence of weight matrices. If there exists a positive number μ such that every entry of every W_i, $i = 1, 2, \ldots$ is at least as large as μ, then the sequence of products W_1, $W_2 W_1$, ... converges to consensus.*

The above convergence condition may, in fact, be weakened considerably. Note that for any $\mu > 0$, the sequence of sums $\mu, \mu + \mu = 2\mu, \mu + \mu + \mu = 3\mu$, ... increases without bound, or in mathematical terminology, diverges to $+\infty$. This suggests the following generalization of Theorem 8.2:

THEOREM 8.3. *Let W_1, W_2, ... be a sequence if weight matrices and for each $i \geqslant 1$, let μ_i denote the smallest entry of W_i. If the sequence of sums μ_1, $\mu_1 + \mu_2$, ... diverges to $+\infty$, then the sequence of products W_1, $W_2 W_1$, ... converges to consensus.*

A proof of Theorem 8.3 appears in a technical appendix at the end of this chapter. Note that the numbers μ_i need not all be positive. Indeed, an infinite number of the μ_i's might be equal to zero, consistent with satisfying the hypothesis of the above theorem. The sequence $\mu_1, \mu_2, \ldots$ may even converge to zero, as in the case $\mu_i = 1/i$, which, as is well known, gives rise to the divergent "harmonic series" $1 + 1/2 + 1/3 + \ldots$. On the other hand, this convergence may not occur too rapidly. If, for example, $\mu_i = 1/2^i$, the resulting geometric series $1/2 + 1/4 + 1/8 + \ldots$ converges to the finite limit 1, and so this set of lower bounds does not satisfy the hypothesis of Theorem 8.3. See also Seneta and Chatterjee [1977].

As one might expect from Theorem 7.2 the conditions posited in Theorem 8.3 are by no means necessary for convergence to consensus in the extended case. Indeed, it is possible that every matrix in the sequence $W_1, W_2, \ldots$ contains at least one zero entry and yet the sequence of products $W_1, W_2 W_1$ converges to consensus. It is beyond the scope of our interests to attempt to describe the most general set of conditions under which convergence to consensus obtains. We content ourselves with the statement of an extended convergence theorem which has something of the flavor of Theorem 7.2:

THEOREM 8.4. *Let* $W_1, W_2, \ldots$ *by a sequence of weight matrices and let* i_1, $i_2, \ldots$ *be some increasing sequence of positive integers. Define a sequence of* "*block*" *products* $U_1, U_2, \ldots$ *by* $U_1 = W_{i_1} W_{i_1 - 1} \ldots W_1$, $U_2 = W_{i_2} W_{i_2 - 1}$ $\ldots W_{i_1 + 1}$, *etc. Let* β_i *denote the smallest entry of* U_i, $i = 1, 2, \ldots$. *If* β_1, $\beta_1 + \beta_2, \ldots$ *diverges to* $+ \infty$, *then the sequence of product* $W_1, W_2 W_1, \ldots$ *converges to consensus.*

A proof of Theorem 8.4, which follows quickly from Theorem 8.3, appears in the technical appendix at the end of this chapter. The parameters β_i are lower bounds on respect communicated across possibly more than one level of judgmental skill. If the numbers β_i are of sufficient magnitude to satisfy the hypothesis of Theorem 8.4, then there are chains of respect (of a much more complex sort than those in the elementary case) implicit in the matrices W_1, $W_2, \ldots$ which are sufficient to yield convergence to consensus.

3. HIERARCHIES OF DECISIONMAKING GROUPS

We now generalize the results of the preceding section by dropping the assumption that a single group of individuals is responsible for the evaluation of judgmental skills at all levels. Thus we shall suppose that a group G_0 of n_0 individuals evaluates the initial decision variable and attempts to arrive at consensus. If this group fails to reach consensus, a group G_1 of n_1 individuals attempts to determine a consensual set of weights with which to average the opinions of members of the first group. If consensus on these weights is not achieved by G_1, a group G_2 of n_2 individuals seeks a consensual set of weights with which to average the weights chosen by members of G_1, etc.

Thus G_0 produces an $n_0 \times 1$ column matrix A, G_1 an $n_1 \times n_0$ weight matrix W_1, G_2 an $n_2 \times n_1$ weight matrix W_2, etc. In general, for each positive integer k, there may be a group G_k which produces an $n_k \times n_{k-1}$ weight matrix W_k which reflects the respect of individuals in G_k for individuals in G_{k-1} as evaluators of individuals in G_{k-2}. We assume that the individuals in G_k are assigned labels $I_1^{(k)}, I_2^{(k)}, \ldots, I_{n_k}^{(k)}$ and that the entry $w_{ij}^{(k)}$ of W_k expresses the opinion of $I_i^{(k)}$ as to the weight deserved by $I_j^{(k-1)}$ as an evaluator of individuals in G_{k-2}. We do not stipulate any set-theoretic relations among these groups — they may be identical, disjoint, or partly overlapping. Moreover, if an individual belongs to more than one group, the subscripts on his group labels need not match.

As in the preceding section, the row sums associated with these weight matrices are always unitary. But the elementary sequence of powers W, W^2, ... and its companion sequence A, WA, W^2A, ... is replaced by a sequence of products W_1, $W_2 W_1$, $(W_3 W_2)W_1$, ... and a companion sequence $W_1 A$, $(W_2 W_1)A$, $((W_3 W_2)W_1)A$, ..., where the row dimensions of the products in the latter two sequences may vary — W_1 is $n_1 \times n_0$, $W_2 W_1$ is $n_2 \times n_0$, $W_1 A$ is $n_1 \times 1$, $(W_2 W_1)A$ is $n_2 \times 1$, etc. A typical entry of one of these products summarizes a certain amount of information bearing on the problem at hand. Thus, for example, the i-th entry of $(W_2 W_1)A$ is the value of the initial decision variable that one would accept if one took into account the complete set of opinions of individuals in G_0 regarding this value, and the complete set of evaluations of individuals in G_0 by those in G_1, the latter weighted by the opinions of the single individual $I_i^{(2)}$ of G_2 as to the expertise of members of G_1.

Many of the properties of matrix powers mentioned in the previous chapter carry over to the more general setting of matrix products. For example, if W_k is a consensus matrix, then $W_k W_{k-1} \ldots W_1$ will be consensus matrix.[1] Moreover, if $W_k W_{k-1} \ldots W_1$ is a consensus matrix, then $W_{k+1} W_k W_{k-1} \ldots W_1$ is a consensus matrix, each column of which is identical with the corresponding column of $W_k W_{k-1} \ldots W_1$, except perhaps in length. More generally, the individual entries in a given column of $W_{k+1} W_k W_{k-1} \ldots W_1$ lie between the largest and smallest entries of the corresponding column of $W_k W_{k-1} \ldots W_1$. Hence, if $W_k W_{k-1} \ldots W_1$ is what we have called an ϵ-consensus matrix, so too will be $W_{k+1} W_k W_{k-1} \ldots W_1$.

Since the row dimensions of $W_k W_{k-1} \ldots W_1$ may vary with k, we cannot talk of convergence of a sequence of such products to some fixed consensual weight matrix L. There is, however, a clear sense in which there may be a set of weights $\lambda_1, \lambda_2, \ldots, \lambda_{n_0}$ which are rationally accorded to individuals in G_0 in virtue of amalgamating the total available information relevant to this issue. For, suppose that for each $\epsilon > 0$, there is a positive integer k_ϵ such that for for all $k \geqslant k_\epsilon$ and all $j = 1, 2, \ldots, n_0$ the absolute values of the differences between λ_j and any element of the jth column of $W_k W_{k-1} \ldots W_1$ are uniformly bounded above by ϵ. In such a case we might say that the sequence of products $W_1, W_2 W_1, \ldots$ is "column-convergent" to consensus. This is clearly the proper generalization of the notion of convergence to this more general setting and one may check easily that the proofs of Theorem 8.1, 8.2, 8.3, and 8.4 go through in this setting modulo a simple change of terminology from "convergent" to "column convergent."

4. CONSENSUS BY OTHER MEANS

In Chapter Six we encountered averaging functions other than weighted arithmetic means and saw that at least one such class of functions, the weighted geometric means, provides an appropriate aggregation method for a certain type of social choice problem. However, whether weighted arithmetic or geometric means were the method of aggregation under consideration, the consensual weights involved in their specification were assumed to emerge from the iterated *arithmetic* averaging described in this chapter and the preceding one. As noted in Chapter 6, this special role of arithmetic averaging is understandable in terms of Theorem 6.4, for the determination of such weights is an allocation problem. In the present section we show how iterated arithmetic averaging emerges in a natural way in the determination of consensual weights, even when some other type of iterated averaging is employed to determine consensual values of the initial decision variable.

We begin with a simple example, involving a decisionmaking group with two individuals. We suppose that their opinions as to the most appropriate value of some decision variable are represented by a column matrix $A = [a_1, a_2]^T$. We suppose also that the individuals grant each other uniform respect at all levels of judgment, as expressed by the 2×2 weight matrix $W = (w_{ij})$. In Chapter 7 we saw how the associativity of matrix multiplication enabled us to view the sequence $A, WA, W(WA), W(W(WA)), \ldots$ of modifications of A as $A, WA, W^2 A, W^3 A, \ldots$ and hence to investigate convergence of the original sequence in terms of convergence of powers of W.

Suppose, however, that this group thought it appropriate to modify A by iterated geometric averaging. Then

$$W * A = \begin{bmatrix} w_{11} & w_{12} \\ w_{21} & w_{22} \end{bmatrix} * \begin{bmatrix} a_1 \\ a_2 \end{bmatrix} = \begin{bmatrix} w_{11} & w_{12} \\ a_1 \cdot a_2 \\ w_{21} & w_{22} \\ a_1 \cdot a_2 \end{bmatrix} = $$

would express the first modification of A, and

$$W * (W * A) = \begin{bmatrix} w_{11} & w_{12} \\ w_{21} & w_{22} \end{bmatrix} * \begin{bmatrix} w_{11} & w_{12} \\ a_1 \cdot a_2 \\ w_{21} & w_{22} \\ a_1 \cdot a_2 \end{bmatrix} = $$

$$= \begin{bmatrix} a_1^{w_{11} w_{11} + w_{12} w_{21}} \cdot a_2^{w_{11} w_{12} + w_{12} w_{22}} \\ a_1^{w_{21} w_{11} + w_{22} w_{21}} \cdot a_2^{w_{21} w_{12} + w_{32} w_{22}} \end{bmatrix}$$

the second modification. Note that the composition $*$ is not associative. We do not have $W * (W * A) = (W * W) * A$, but rather, $W * (W * A) = W^2 * A$, where W^2 indicates, as usual, the ordinary matrix product WW. Indeed, as shown below, the sequence A, $W * A$, $W * (W * A)$, $W * (W * (W (A)))$, ... of repeated geometric modifications of A is identical with the sequence A, $W * A$, $W^2 * A$, $W^3 * A$, ... If the sequence W, W^2, W^3, ... of ordinary powers of W converges to a consensus matrix with identical rows (λ_1, λ_2), then repeated geometric modifications of A converge to a consensual column matrix with identical entries $a_1^{\lambda_1} a_2^{\lambda_2}$.

Moreover, the above result holds for a rather wide class of averaging functions. Let us call a function $f: S \to R$, where $S \subseteq R^n$, a *quasi-arithmetic averaging function* if there is a strictly monotonic[2] function g, defined on an appropriate subset S of R^n, and a sequence of weights $w_1, w_2, \ldots, w_n$ with $0 \leq w_i \leq 1$ and $w_1 + w_2 + \ldots + w_n = 1$, such that $f(x_1, x_2, \ldots, x_n) = g^{-1}(w_1 g(x_1) + w_2 g(x_2) + \ldots + w_n g(x_n))$ for all $(x_1, x_2, \ldots, x_n) \in S$. The class of quasi-arithmetic averaging functions is infinite, and includes the following familiar functions:

(i)   weighted arithmetic means $(S = R^n, g(x) = x)$;
(ii) weighted geometric means $(S = \{(x_1, x_2, \ldots, x_n) \in R: x_i > 0\}$, $g(x) = \log x)$;
(iii) weighted harmonic means $(S = \{(x_1, x_2, \ldots, x_n) \in R^n: x_i > 0\}$, $g(x) = 1/x)$.[3]

The following theorem shows that the situation noted above for iterated geometric averaging obtains more generally in the case of iterated quasi-arithmetic averaging:

THEOREM 8.5. *Let g be a strictly monotonic function, with inverse g^{-1}. Let $B = (b_i)$ be an $n \times 1$ column matrix and $W = (w_{ij})$ an $m \times n$ weight matrix, and denote by $W * B = (b_i')$ the $m \times 1$ column matrix such that $b_i' = g^{-1}(w_{i1} g(b_1) + w_{i2} g(b_2) + \ldots + w_{in} g(b_n))$. Then if A is any $n_0 \times 1$ column matrix, W_1 an $n_1 \times n_0$ weight matrix, and W_2 an $n_2 \times n_1$ weight matrix, $W_2 * (W_1 * A) = (W_2 W_1) * A$, where $W_2 W_1$ denotes the ordinary matrix product of W_2 with W_1.*

Since the proof of the foregoing theorem is short, we present it immediately, rather than relegating it to the technical appendix.

Proof. For any matrix B, denote by $g(B)$ (respectively, $g^{-1}(B)$) the matrix which results from applying g (respectively, g^{-1}) to every entry of B. Now, by definition; $W_1 * A = g^{-1}(W_1 g(A))$, where $W_1 g(A)$ denotes the ordinary matrix product of W_1 with $g(A)$. Hence, $W_2 * (W_1 * A) = g^{-1}(W_2 g(W_1 * A)) = g^{-1}(W_2 g(g^{-1}(W_1 g(A)))) = g^{-1}(W_2 W_1 g(A)) = (W_2 W_1) * A$.

It follows by induction from the above theorem that a sequence A, $W_1 * A$, $W_2 * (W_1 * A)$, $W_3 * (W_2 * (W_1 * A))$, ... of modifications of a matrix A by iterated quasi-arithmetic averaging is identical with the sequence A, $W_1 * A$, $(W_2 W_1) * A$, $(W_3 W_2 W_1) * A$, ... Hence convergence of the ordinary products W_1, $W_2 W_1$, $W_3 W_2 W_1$, ... to consensus insures convergence to a consensual value of the initial decision variable, so long as the function g is continuous.

With this ultimate generalization of the elementary model, we rest our case for the cogency of matrix models of consensus.

5. TECHNICAL APPENDIX

The proof of Theorem 8.3 is based on the following two lemmas:

LEMMA 1. *Let μ_1, μ_2, ... be a sequence of real numbers such that $0 \leqslant \mu_i < 1$ for all $i \geqslant 1$. Then the sequence of products $(1-\mu_1)$, $(1-\mu_2)(1-\mu_1)$, $(1-\mu_3)(1-\mu_2)(1-\mu_1)$, ... converges to zero if and only if the sequence of sums μ_1, $\mu_1 + \mu_2$, $\mu_1 + \mu_2 + \mu_3$, ... diverges to ∞.*

The proof of Lemma 1 appears in Isaacson and Madsen [1976, p. 37].

LEMMA 2. *Let W_1 and W_2 be $n \times n$ weight matrices, $n \geq 2$, and let μ_i denote the smallest entry of W_i, $i = 1, 2$. Then the differences between the largest and smallest elements of each of the columns of $W_2 W_1$ are uniformly bounded above by $(1-2\mu_2)(1-2\mu_1)$.*

Proof. The proof of this lemma involves a straightforward generalization of the core argument of the classical proof of convergence of powers of a regular weight matrix. See Kemeny and Snell [1976]. Denote a typical entry of W_1 by $w_{ij}^{(1)}$ and a typical entry of W_2 by $w_{ij}^{(2)}$. Let

$$(1) \qquad w_{ij}^* = w_{i1}^{(2)} w_{1j}^{(1)} + w_{i2}^{(2)} w_{2j}^{(1)} + \ldots + w_{in}^{(2)} w_{nj}^{(1)}$$

denote the ith entry of the jth column of $W_2 W_1$. Let m_j denote the smallest entry of the jth column of W_1 and M_j the largest entry in that column, and let m_j' denote the smallest entry in the jth column of $W_2 W_1$ and M_j' the largest entry in that column. Suppose that $w_{tj}^{(1)} = m_j$ and $w_{sj}^{(1)} = M_j$. If, in expression (1) above, we replace all of the numbers $w_{1j}^{(1)}$, $w_{2j}^{(1)}$, ..., $w_{nj}^{(1)}$, except for $w_{tj}^{(1)} = m_j$, by M_j, the resulting sum has the value $w_{it}^{(2)} m_j + (1 - w_{it}^{(2)}) M_j = M_j - w_{it}^{(2)} (M_j - m_j)$ and this number is greater than or equal to w_{ij}^*. Hence

$$M_j' \leqslant M_j - w_{it}^{(2)} (M_j - m_j), \text{ and since } w_{it}^{(2)} \geqslant \mu_2,$$

$$(2) \qquad M_j' \leqslant M_j - \mu_2 (M_j - m_j).$$

Similarly, if, in expression (1) above, we replace all of the numbers

$$w_{1j}^{(1)}, w_{2j}^{(1)}, \ldots, w_{nj}^{(1)}, \text{ except for } w_{sj}^{(1)} = M_j, \text{ by } m_j, \text{ the}$$

resulting sum has the value $w_{is}^{(2)} M_j + (1 - w_{is}^{(2)}) m_j = m_j + w_{is}^{(2)} (M_j - m_j)$, and this number is less than or equal to w_{ij}^*. Hence,

$$m_j' \geqslant m_j + w_{is}^{(2)} (M_j - m_j), \text{ and since } w_{is}^{(2)} \geqslant \mu_2,$$

$$(3) \qquad m_j' \geqslant m_j + \mu_2 (M_j - m_j).$$

It now follows from (2) and (3) that

$$(4) \qquad M_j' - m_j' \leqslant (1-2\mu_2)(M_j - m_j).$$

But $m_j \geqslant \mu_1$ and $M_j \leqslant 1-\mu_1$ (for since $n \geqslant 2$, there is at least one entry other than M_j in the same row as that of any occurrence of M_j. This entry is at least as large as μ_1, and so $M_j \leqslant 1-\mu_1$, since row sums are unitary.) It follows that $M_j - m_j \leqslant (1-2\mu_1)$ and hence that

$$(5) \qquad M_j' - m_j' \leqslant (1-2\mu_2)(1-2\mu_1)$$

for $j = 1, 2, \ldots, n$, which completes the proof.

Now the above argument can be iterated to apply to products of more than two weight matrices. Thus, if W_3 is an $n \times n$ matrix with smallest element μ_3, and M_j'' denotes the largest element in the jth column of $W_3 W_2 W_1$ and m_j'' the smallest element of that column, it follows from (4) and (5) that $M_j'' - m_j'' \leqslant (1-2\mu_3)(M_j' - m_j') \leqslant (1-2\mu_3)(1-2\mu_2)(1-2\mu_1)$ for $j = 1, 2, \ldots, n$. This, along with the crucial nesting property $[m_j, M_j] \supseteq [m_j', M_j'] \supseteq [m_j'', M_j''] \supseteq \ldots$, makes it clear that the sequence of products $W_1, W_2 W_1, W_3 W_2 W_1, \ldots$ converges to consensus whenever $(1-2\mu_1), (1-2\mu_2)(1-2\mu_1), (1-2\mu_3)(1-2\mu_2)(1-2\mu_1), \ldots$ converges to zero.

But by Lemma 1, the latter condition is equivalent to the divergence of the sequence, $2\mu_1, 2\mu_1 + 2\mu_2, 2\mu_1 + 2\mu_2 + 2\mu_3, \ldots$ to $+\infty$, and this in turn is clearly equivalent to the divergence of the sequence $\mu_1, \mu_1 + \mu_2, \mu_1 + \mu_2 + \mu_3, \ldots$ to $+\infty$. This proves

THEOREM 8.3. *Let* W_1, W_2, ... *be a sequence of weight matrices and for each* $i \geqslant 1$, *let* μ_i *denote the smallest element of* W_i. *If the sequence of sums* $\mu_1, \mu_1 + \mu_2, \ldots$ *diverges to* $+\infty$, *then the sequence of products* $W_1, W_2 W_1$, *... converges to consensus.*

It is a simple matter to extend the above result to

THEOREM 8.4. *Let* W_1, W_2, ... *be a sequence of weight matrices and let* $i_1, i_2, i_3, \ldots$ *be some increasing sequence of positive integers. Define a sequence of "block" products* $U_1 = W_{i_1} W_{i_1 - 1} \ldots W_1$, $U_2 = W_{i_2} W_{i_2 - 1} \ldots W_{i_1 + 1}$, *etc. Let* β_i *denote the smallest entry of the matrix* U_i. *If* $\beta_1, \beta_1 + \beta_2, \ldots$ *diverges to* $+\infty$, *then the sequence of products* $W_1, W_2 W_1$, *converges to consensus.*

Proof. It follows immediately from Theorem 8.3 that the sequence of products $U_1, U_2 U_1, \ldots$ converges to consensus. This fact, combined with what we have called the "nesting property" of weighted arithmetic averaging, yields the convergence of the sequence $W_1, W_2 W_1, W_3 W_2 W_1, \ldots$ to consensus. For by this nesting property, it suffices to show that for all $\epsilon > 0$, there is a positive integer k_ϵ such that, for all $k > k_\epsilon$, $W_k W_{k-1} \ldots W_1$ is an ϵ-consensus matrix. By the convergence of $U_1, U_2 U_1, \ldots$ to consensus, there is a positive integer r_ϵ such that for all $r > r_\epsilon$, $U_r U_{r-1} \ldots U_1$ is an ϵ-consensus matrix. But $U_r U_{r-1} \ldots U_1 = W_{i_r} W_{i_r - 1} \ldots W_1$. Hence, when $r > r_\epsilon$, $W_{i_r} W_{i_r - 1} \ldots W_1$ is an ϵ-consensus matrix, and since further multiplication by weight matrices on the left by this product preserves ϵ-consensus, it follows that $W_k W_{k-1} \ldots W_1$ is an ϵ-consensus matrix when $k > i_{r_\epsilon}$.

NOTES

[1] In particular, if G_k consists of a single individual, W_k will always be a consensus matrix. Note, moreover, that the term "consensus," applied to a matrix product W_k $W_{k-1} \ldots W_1$, has a broader connotation than in the previous chapter. If the groups G_0, $G_1 \ldots$ are not identical, what we call consensus may not carry the explicit endorsement of all individuals involved in the decision-making process. For individuals may be called on to offer opinions regarding just one component of relevant information. Nevertheless, an individual's willingness to participate in a possibly limited way in the determination of the initial decision variable implies a general respect for this decision-making format and for the other groups involved in it. An individual in G_k having no respect for an individual in G_{k-1} can assign that individual the weight 0. He does not have that option with respect to individuals in G_{k+1}, G_{k+2}, etc. On the other hand, he can refuse to participate if this is objectionable to him.

[2] A function is strictly monotonic if it is strictly increasing or strictly decreasing. Such functions are $1-1$, and hence invertible. We require g to be strictly monotonic, so that a quasi-arithmetic average of a sequence of numbers will lie between the smallest and the largest of these numbers. Suppose, for example that g, and hence g^{-1}, is strictly decreasing. Then

$$\min \{x_i\} \leqslant g^{-1} (w_1 g(x_1) + w_2 g(x_2) + \ldots + w_n g(x_n)) \leqslant \max \{x_i\}.$$

For

$$g(\min \{x_i\}) \geqslant g(x_i) \geqslant g(\max \{x_i\}), \text{ and so}$$

$$g(\min \{x_i\}) \geqslant w_i g(x_1) + w_2 g(x_2) + \ldots + w_n g(x_n) \geqslant g(\max \{x_i\}),$$

and

$$\min \{x_i\} = g^{-1} (g(\min \{x_i\})) \leqslant g^{-1} (w_1 g(x_1) + w_2 g(x_2) + \ldots + w_n g(x_n)) \leqslant g^{-1} (g(\max \{x_i\})) = \max \{x_i\}.$$

The proof for strictly increasing g is similar.

[3] More generally, we may take

$$S = \{(x_1, x_2, \ldots, x_n) \in R^n : x_i > 0\}$$

and $g(x) = x^p$ for some nonzero $p \in R$, whence $g^{-1}(x) = x^{1/p}$, and

$$f(x_1, x_2, \ldots, x_n) = (w_1 x_1^p + w_2 x_2^p + \ldots + w_n x_n^p)^{1/p}.$$

When $p = -1$, we get the weighted harmonic mean. When $p = 2$, we get a weighted "root-mean-square."

REFERENCES

Aczél, J.: 1966, *Lectures on Functional Equations* (Academic Press, New York).

Aczél, J. and Wagner C.: 1980, 'A characterization of weighted arithmetic means', *SIAM Journal of Algebraic and Discrete Methods* 1, pp. 259–260.

Aczél, J., Kannappan, P. and Ng, C. T.: 'Rational group decision-making revisited: a more natural characterization of arithmetic means', to appear.

Arrow, Kenneth J.: 1951, Second Edition, 1963, *Social Choice and Individual Values*, Cowles Commission Monograph 12 (John Wiley and Sons, New York).

Arrow, Kenneth J.: 1977, 'Extended sympathy and the possibility of social choice', *The American Economic Review* 89, pp. 219–225.

Barry, Brian: 1973, *The Liberal Theory of Justice* (Oxford University Press, Oxford).

Bentham, Jeremy: 1789, *The Principles of Morals and Legislation*.

Berman, A. and Plemmons, R. J.: 1979, *Nonnegative Matrices in the Mathematical Sciences* (Academic Press, New York).

Blackwell, D. and Girshick, G. H.: 1954, *Theory of Games and Statistical Decisions* (John Wiley and Sons, New York).

Carnap, Rudolf: 1963, *The Logical Foundations of Probability*, Second Edition (University of Chicago Press, Chicago).

Chisholm, Roderick M.: 1977, *Theory of Knowledge*, Second Edition (Prentice-Hall, Englewood Cliffs).

Cohen, L. Jonathan: 1976, *The Probable and the Provable* (Clarendon Press, Oxford).

d'Aspremont, Claude and Gevers, Louis: 1977, 'Equity and the informational basis of collective choice', *Review of Economic Studies* 46, pp. 199–210.

DeGroot, Morris H.: 1974, 'Reaching a consensus', *Journal of the American Statistical Association* 69, pp. 118–212.

Dickie, R. H.: 1974, 'The oblateness of the Sun and relativity', *Science* 184, pp. 419–429.

Doob, J. L.: 1953, *Stochastic Processes* (John Wiley and Sons, New York).

Duhem, Pierre: 1954, *The Aim and Structure of Physical Theory*, (Princeton University, Princeton).

Eisenberg, E. and Gale, D.: 1959, 'Consensus of subjective probabilities: the pari-mutuel method', *Annals of Mathematical Statistics* 30, pp. 165–168.

Feinberg, Joel: 1974, 'The rights of animals and unborn generations', in *Philosophy and Environmental Crisis*, W. T. Blackstone (ed.), (University of Georgia Press, Athens).

Frankfurt, Harry: 1971, 'Freedom of the will and the concept of person', *Journal of Philosophy* 68, pp. 5–20.

French, John R. P., Jr.: 1956, 'A formal theory of social power', *Psychological Review* 63, pp. 181–194.

Gettier, Edmund L. Jr.: 1963, 'Is justified true belief knowledge?', *Analysis* 23, pp. 121–123.

Gevers, Louis: 1979, 'On interpersonal comparability and social welfare orderings', *Econometrica* 47, pp. 75–89.

Goodman, Nelson: 1955, *Pact, Fiction and Forecast* (Harvard University Press, Cambridge).

Grice, H. P.: 1969, 'Utterer's meaning and intentions', *Philosophical Review* 82, pp. 147–177.

Grice, H. P.: 1975, 'Logic and conversation', in *Syntax and Semantics*, Vol 3, P. Cole and J. L. Morgan (eds.), (Academic Press, New York), pp. 43–58.

Harary, F.: 1959, 'A criterion for unanimity in French's theory of social power', in *Studies in Social Power*, ed. by D. Cartwright (Institute for Social Research, Ann Arbon, Mich.), pp. 168–182.

Harsanyi, John C.: 1976, *Essays on Ethics, Social Behavior and Scientific Explanation* (D. Reidel, Dordrecht, Holland).

Harsanyi, John C.: 1977, *Rational Behavior and Bargaining Equilibrium in Games and Social Situations* (Cambridge University Press, New York).

Helmer, Olaf: 1963, 'The systematic use of expert judgment in operations research', P-2795 (The RAND Corporation, Santa Monica).

Helmer, Olaf and Brown, Bernice: 1964, 'Improving the reliability of estimates obtained from a consensus of experts', P-2086 (The RAND Corporation, Santa Monica).

Hempel, Carl G.: 1962, 'Deductive-nomological vs. statistical explanation', in *Minnesota Studies in the Philosophy of Science* III, H. Feigl and G. Maxwell (eds.), (University of Minnesota Press, Minneapolis).

Hill, H. A. and Caudell, T. P.: 1977, 'Solar oscillations in the 1973 oblateness observations', *Bulletin of the American Astronomical Society* 9, p. 357.

Hilpinen, Risto: 1968, *Rules of Acceptance and Inductive Logic, Acta Philosophica Fennica* XXII (North-Holland, Amsterdam).

Hintikka, Jaakko: 1966, 'A two-dimensional continuum of inductive methods', in *Aspects of Inductive Logic*, Jaakko Hintikka and Patrick Suppes (eds.), (North-Holland, Amsterdam), pp. 113–132.

Hintikka, Jaakko, and Pietarinen, J.: 1966, 'Semantic information and inductive logic', in *Aspects of Inductive Logic*, Jaakko Hintikka and Patrick Suppes (eds.), (North-Holland, Amsterdam).

Hobbes, Thomas: 1651, *Leviathan*.

Isaacson, Dean L. and Madsen, Richard W.: 1975, *Markov Chains: Theory and Applications* (John Wiley and Sons, New York).

Isaacson, D. and Madsen R.: (1974), 'Positive columns for stochastic matrices', *Journal of Applied Probability* 11, pp. 829–835.

Jeffrey, Richard C.: 1965, *The Logic of Decision* (McGraw-Hill, New York).

Jeffrey, Richard C.: 1970, 'Dracula meets Wolfman: Acceptance vs. partial belief', in *Induction, Acceptance, and Rational Belief*, Marshall Swain (ed.), (D. Reidel, Dordrecht, Holland), pp. 157–185.

Jeffrey, Richard C.: 1974, 'Preferences among preferences', *Journal of Philosophy* 71, pp. 377–391.

Kant, Immanuel: 1785, *Foundations of the Metaphysics of Morals*.

Kemeny, John G. and Snell, J. Laurie: 1976, *Finite Markov Chains* (Springer-Verlag, New York).

Kripke, Saul: 1972, 'Naming and necessity', in *Semantics of Natural Languages*, Donald Davidson and Gilbert Harman (eds.), (D. Reidel, Dordrecht, Holland), pp. 253–355.

Lehrer, Adrienne: 1974, *Semantic Fields and Lexical Structures*, (North-Holland, Amsterdam).

Lehrer, Adrienne: 1975, 'Talking about wine', *Language* 51, pp. 901–923.

Lehrer, Keith: 1974, 'Truth, evidence, and inference', *American Philosophical Quarterly* 11, pp. 79–92.

Lehrer, Keith: 1976, 'Induction, consensus and catastrophe', in *Local Induction*, Radu J. Bogdan (ed.), (D. Reidel, Dordrecht, Holland), pp. 115–143.

Lehrer, Keith: 1976a, 'When rational disagreement is impossible', *Noûs* 10, pp. 327–332.

Lehrer, Keith: 1977, 'Social information', *The Monist* 60, pp. 473–487.

Lehrer, Keith: 1978, 'Consensus and comparison: A theory of social rationality', in *Foundations and Applications of Decision Theory*, Vol. 1, C. A. Hooker, J. J. Leach, and E. F. McClennen (eds.), (D. Reidel, Dordrecht, Holland).

Levi, Isaac: 1967, *Gambling with Truth* (Alfred A. Knopf, New York).

Lewis, David: 1969, *Convention* (Harvard University, Cambridge).

Locke, John: 1690, *Second Treatise of Government*.

Locke, John: 1690a, *Essay Concerning Human Understanding*.

McConway, K. J.: 'Marginalisation and linear opinion pools', to appear.

Mill, John Stuart: 1863, *Utilitarianism*.

Moore, George E.: 1922, *Philosophical Studies* (Routledge and Kegan Paul, London).

Moore, George E.: 1956, *Principia Ethica* (Cambridge University Press, Cambridge).

Nozick, Robert: 1974, *Anarchy, State and Utopia* (Basic Books, New York).

Popper, Karl R.: 1963, *Conjectures and Refutations* (Routledge and Kegan Paul, London).

Putnam, Hilary: 1973, 'Meaning and reference', *Journal of Philosophy* 70, pp. 699–711.

Quine, Willard van Orman: 1960, *Word and Object* (John Wiley and Sons, New York).

Ramsey, Frank. P.: 1931, 'Truth and probability', in Ramsey's *The Foundations of Mathematics and Other Essays*, R. B. Braithwaite (ed.), (Routledge and Kegan Paul, London).

Rawls, John: 1971, *A Theory of Justice* (Harvard, Cambridge).

Reichenbach, Hans: 1949, *The Theory of Probability*, Second Edition (University of California).

Reid, Thomas: 1764, *Inquiry into the Human Mind*.

Reid, Thomas: 1785, *Essays on the Intellectual Powers*.

Roberts, Fred S.: 1976, *Discrete Mathematical Models* (Prentice-Hall, Englewood Cliffs, N.J.).

Roberts, Fred S.: 1979, *Measurement Theory* (Addison-Wesley, Reading, Mass.).

Rousseau, Jean Jacques: 1762, *The Social Contract*.

Saaty, Thomas L.: 1977, 'A scaling method for priorities in hierarchical structures', *Journal of Mathematical Psychology* 15, pp. 234–281.

Sanders, Frederick: 1963, 'On subjective probability forecasting', *Journal of Applied Meteorology* 2, pp. 191–201.

Savage, Leonard J.: 1954, *Foundations of Statistics* (John Wiley and Sons, New York).

Sellars, Wilfrid: 1974, *Essays in Philosophy and Its History* (D. Reidel, Dordrecht, Holland).

Sen, Amartya: 1977, 'Social choice theory: a re-examination', *Econometrica* 45, pp. 53–89.

Seneta, E. and Chatterjee, S.: 1977, 'Towards consensus: Some convergence theorems on repeated averaging', *Journal of Applied Probability* 14, pp. 89–97.

Shiffer, S.: 1972, *Meaning* (Clarendon Press, Oxford).

Skyrms, Brian: 1980, *Causal Necessity* (Yale University, New Haven).

Spinoza, Baruch: 1677, *Ethics*.

Stone, M.: 1961, 'The opinion pool', *Annals of Mathematical Statistics* 32, pp. 1339–1342.

Strasnick, Steven: 1976, 'The problem of social choice: Arrow to Rawls', *Philosophy and Public Affairs* 5, No. 3.

Strasnick, Steven: 1979, 'Moral structures and axiomatic theory', *Theory and Decision* 11, pp. 195–206.

Wagner, Carl: 1978, 'Consensus through respect: A model of rational group decision-making', *Philosophical Studies* 34, pp. 335–349.

Wagner, Carl: 1981a, 'The formal foundations of Lehrer's theory of consensus', in PROFILE: *Keith Lehrer*, Radu J. Bogdan (ed.), (D. Reidel, Dordrecht, Holland).

Wagner, Carl: 1981b, 'Allocation, Lehrer models, and the consensus of probabilities', *Theory and Decision*, to appear.

Winkler, Robert L.: 1969, 'The consensus of subjective probability distributions', *Management Science* 15, pp. B-61–B-75.

Wolff, Robert Paul: 1977, *Understanding Rawls* (Princeton University Press, Princeton).

INDEX OF NAMES

158

INDEX OF SUBJECTS

Printed in the United States
60215LVS00002B/304